Comparable Worth

Comparable Worth

IS IT A WORTHY POLICY?

✣

Elaine Sorensen

PRINCETON UNIVERSITY PRESS

PRINCETON, NEW JERSEY

Library of Congress Cataloging-in-Publication Data

Sorensen, Elaine, 1955–
Comparable worth: is it a worthy policy? / Elaine Sorensen.
p.   cm.
Includes bibliographical references and index.
ISBN 0-691-03263-7 (acid-free)
1. Pay equity—United States. I. Title.
HD6061.2.U6S678   1994
331.2'153'0973—dc20   93-23874

This book has been composed in Laser Caledonia

Princeton University Press books are
printed on acid-free paper and meet the guidelines
for permanence and durability of the Committee
on Production Guidelines for Book Longevity
of the Council on Library Resources

Printed in the United States of America

1   3   5   7   9   10   8   6   4   2

TO BARBARA SORENSEN

✢

✣ Contents ✣

❖ *Figures* ❖

❖ *Tables* ❖

❖ *Acknowledgments* ❖

My INITIAL DEBT goes to Lloyd Ulman and Clair Brown, who taught me labor economics while in graduate school. Their combined expertise provided me with a rich understanding of labor issues, which has influenced my views ever since. I am also greatly indebted to Lee Bawden, who suggested that I write this book. He gave me the opportunity to translate my ideas into a manuscript. Without his encouragement I would not have undertaken this book.

The Urban Institute has provided me with a great research environment during the past six years, for which I am grateful. Many individuals at the Institute have assisted me in this endeavor. Pamela Loprest has been especially wonderful, commenting on numerous revisions of this manuscript and encouraging me through the ups and downs of the review process. John Marcotte helped me understand some of the statistical issues that arose while writing this book. Felicity Skidmore and Kyna Rubin provided detailed comments on earlier drafts of this manuscript, which helped me make the book more accessible. I have also worked with excellent research assistants. In particular, I want to thank Michael Walker and Margaret Weant, both of whom were a pleasure to work with.

Special thanks go to Nancy Gutman, who has believed in me even when I doubted myself. Our friendship has been a source of strength for me for many years. Finally, I want to thank Harold Rennett, my husband, who has stood by me these past six years, through the best and worst of times. His love and support have made it possible for me to complete this project. I dedicate this book to my mother, who almost died last year. She and my father instilled in me a strong sense of independence and compassion, both of which have served me well.

I gratefully acknowledge the financial support for this research, which came from the National Research Council, the Alfred P. Sloan Foundation, and the Ford Foundation.

Comparable Worth

✤

An Overview

Across the country, women working as nurses, librarians, and secretaries argue that their jobs are paid less than jobs of comparable value held primarily by men—that is, jobs requiring comparable skill, effort, responsibility, and working conditions. Many comparisons have been made—nurses to tree trimmers, clerical workers to parking lot attendants—all of which point to a pay discrepancy between "women's work" and "men's work" that cannot be supported by greater job requirements. The state of Minnesota, for example, examined its job classification system and found that Clerk Typists and Delivery Van Drivers were comparable. Yet, in 1981, the maximum salary for Clerk Typists was $267 a month less than that for Delivery Van Drivers. Hence, many women conclude that their work is undervalued because female-dominated jobs tend to be paid less than male-dominated jobs even after accounting for productivity differences in their work.

Many women have turned to comparable worth or pay equity policies as a means to eliminate pay disparities between "women's work" and "men's work" of comparable worth.[1] This doctrine simply states that an employer should pay employees in jobs held predominantly by women the same as employees in jobs held predominantly by men if they require comparable skills, effort, responsibility, and working conditions. Since 1983, the state of Minnesota as well as many other public sector employers have spent millions of dollars to implement comparable worth policies that eliminate these types of pay inequities.

The gender pay gap declined somewhat in the 1980s, but despite these gains women still earn less than men. In 1991, full-time female workers earned only 70 cents for every dollar that full-time male workers earned. This pay disparity persists, in part, because women tend to work in different occupations than men. Three out of five working women are employed in the traditionally female fields of clerical, sales, or service work. Furthermore, most women who work in professional fields are concentrated in two traditionally female occupations: nursing and teaching. Thus, to the extent that "women's work" is underpaid when compared to "men's work" of comparable worth, most female workers experience this type of pay inequity.

During the 1980s, several books were published on the subject of comparable worth, probably the best known of which was published by the National Academy of Sciences titled *Women, Work and Wages: Equal Pay for Jobs of Equal Value*.[2] This book introduced the concept of comparable worth at a time when this policy was still being formulated. In a sense, it helped lay the groundwork for future comparable worth policies. It offered economic justifications for this policy and specific methods for implementing it. Now that ten years have passed, comparable worth policies have been implemented across the country. They have even spread to Canada and other countries around the world. Dozens of studies on the need for comparable worth and its impact have been conducted. This book attempts to update the National Academy of Science's work by reviewing recent studies on the need for and impact of comparable worth policies, as well as offer original research on these subjects.

Changes in Women's Employment Status

Comparable worth initiatives seek to counteract the persistent disparities between male and female pay. Although progress has been made in recent years, women's pay relative to that of men is only six percentage points higher than it was thirty-five years ago. Figure 1.1 shows that the pay ratio of female-to-male earnings for full-time workers peaked in 1955 at 64 percent, after which it gradually declined to 57 percent in 1973, and then it steadily increased, returning to its former level of 64 percent in 1984. Since then the ratio of female-to-male earnings has exceeded its 1955 value.

Severe occupational segregation also characterizes the U.S. labor force. This too has declined somewhat during the past two decades, as table 1.1 indicates. For example, 31 percent of working women now work as managers, professionals, or technical workers, up from 19 percent in 1970. Nonetheless, it is still true that about three out of five working women are employed in clerical, sales, or service work, a figure which has declined only slightly since 1970. In contrast, men are concentrated in an entirely different set of occupations. Two-thirds of men work as managers, professionals, craft workers, or operators.

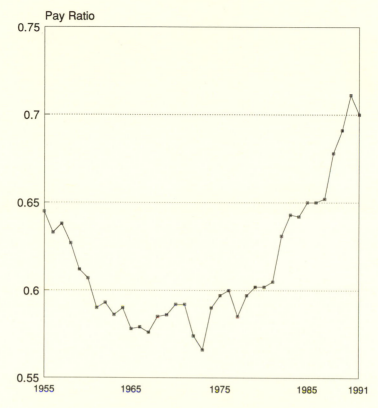

FIGURE 1.1. Ratio of Female to Male Earnings for
Full-Time Workers. Source: U.S. Bureau of the Census,
Current Population Reports, P-60 Series.

These disparities are particularly disturbing given the dramatic
increase in the participation of women in the labor market since
World War II, rising from 33 to 57 percent between 1948 and 1991.[3]
Women are also spending more of their adult lives in the labor force
than ever before. This increased work effort has altered women's
self-perceptions in the United States. Women are now less likely to
think of themselves as temporary employees working for "pin
money." Instead, they anticipate a more permanent attachment to
the labor force and perceive their income as necessary for household
maintenance.

Furthermore, during the past twenty-five years, major federal legislation has been enacted to combat economic discrimination against
women. The Equal Pay Act of 1963 prohibited unequal pay for equal

TABLE 1.1

Percentage Distribution of Women and Men by Major Occupational Groups
for 1970 and 1991

Major Occupational Groups	1970		1991	
	Women	Men	Women	Men
All Occupations	100.0	100.0	100.0	100.0
Managers and Administrators	4.4	14.3	11.4	14.0
Professional and Technicians	14.5	13.9	19.1	15.2
Clerical Workers	34.5	7.1	27.5	5.8
Sales Workers	7.1	5.6	12.8	11.3
Service Workers	21.7	6.7	17.9	10.1
Craft Workers	1.1	20.1	2.1	18.9
Operators and Laborers	14.9	26.9	8.1	20.2
Farming Occupations	1.8	5.3	1.0	4.6

Sources: U.S. Bureau of Labor Statistics, *Employment and Earnings*, January 1992, p. 183; and *Handbook of Labor Statistics*, 1975, p. 71.

Note: The occupational categories for 1970 and 1991 are not strictly comparable. The 1970 data uses the 1960 occupational classification system; the 1991 data uses the 1980 occupational classification system.

work. The Civil Rights Act of 1964 prohibited employment discrimination against women. Then, during President Johnson's administration, women became a protected group under Executive Order 11246, which promotes affirmative action for protected groups among federal contractors. In 1972, Congress passed Title 9 of the Education Amendments, which opened up professional and technical schools to women.[4] These legislative changes have significantly increased the employment opportunities of women.

Nonetheless, despite major employment, attitudinal, and legislative changes, male/female pay disparities and occupational segregation remain largely intact. Proponents of comparable worth argue these changes have been insufficient because of the connection between occupational segregation and women's relative earnings. This point is elaborated below.

THE UNDERPAYMENT OF "WOMEN'S WORK"

Proponents of comparable worth argue that extensive occupational segregation is a major cause of the earnings disparity between women and men.[5] They argue that because of occupational segregation, certain jobs become identified as "women's work." This label results in lower pay, simply because women do the work. Thus, "women's work" is underpaid and this underpayment is a principal reason why women earn less than men. In 1981, the National Academy of Sciences offered evidence to substantiate this view.[6] Using 1970 census data, the authors found that "occupational segregation accounts for about 35–40 percent of the [sex pay] difference."[7] Furthermore, they concluded that "not only do women do different work than men, but also the work women do is paid less, and the more an occupation is dominated by women the less it pays."[8]

Some opponents of comparable worth have interpreted this claim that "women's work" is underpaid to suggest that comparable worth policies would require employers to ascertain a "just" wage for "women's work" based on its inherent value to society. For example, June O'Neill has stated, "By comparable worth I mean the view that employers should base compensation on the inherent value of a job rather than on strictly market considerations. It is not a new idea . . . the concept of the 'just price,' or payment for value."[9] It is not surprising that some have perceived demands for comparable worth in this light, because statements such as "equal pay for work of equal value" sound as if advocates are calling for a "just price" for "women's work."

A more careful reading, however, shows that comparable worth policies are based on relative comparisons of pay and productivity requirements between male- and female-dominated jobs. The purpose of these comparisons is to eliminate the pay disparity between male- and female-dominated jobs that is not accounted for by productivity differences. Concepts such as inherent value or a just price do not reflect the actual intent of comparable worth policies.

The underpayment of "women's work" can be illustrated using data from the annual file of the 1990 Current Population Surveys constructed by the U.S. Bureau of Labor Statistics. Data for full-time workers were aggregated into occupational categories, which were

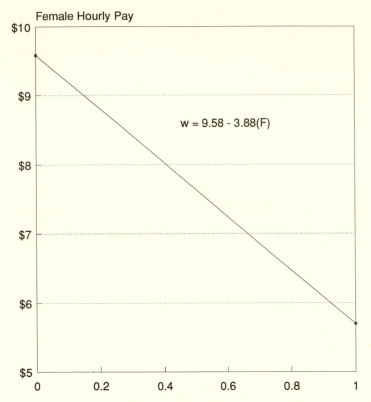

Female Hourly Pay

$$w = 9.58 - 3.88(F)$$

FIGURE 1.2. Female Hourly Pay and the Proportion of
Women in the Occupation. Source: 1990 Current
Population Surveys, annual file.

then ranked according to the average hourly earnings of women in
the occupation with the poorest paid occupation first.[10] Results show
that the poorest paid female-dominated occupation was that of child
care worker, with women holding 97 percent of these jobs. In 1990,
the average hourly pay for full-time female child care workers was
$5.28. The lowest paid male-dominated occupation was that of gas
station attendant. Only 3 percent of the workers in this occupation
were women, and those who worked full time earned an average of
$5.70 an hour. Thus, on average, women earned $0.42 more per hour
working as gas station attendants than as child care workers. Yet, the
mean education completed by women in both of these occupations
was 12 years. Some might find it rather ironic that women pumping

gas made more than women caring for our children. This is one example of the underpayment of female-dominated jobs.

A consistent pattern emerges from this data, which shows that women performing "women's work" earn less than women employed in male-dominated jobs. Multiple regression analysis can be used to estimate the size of this underpayment. The solid line in figure 1.2 shows the relationship between the hourly earnings of women in an occupation and the proportion of workers in that occupation who are women, or F. This line takes into account differences in the amounts of education completed by women in each occupation by including the mean education completed by women in each occupation as an explanatory factor in the regression analysis. These data show that women with twelve years of education working in a job held exclusively by women earn $5.70 per hour. In contrast, women with the same amount of education but working in a job held exclusively by men earn $9.58 per hour. Thus, this analysis finds that working in a female-dominated job reduced a woman's earnings by $3.88 per hour in 1990.[11]

POLICY BACKGROUND

Comparable worth started as a state and local government initiative in the early 1970s. Three principal actors were instrumental in its conception: feminists, the union movement, and state and local government personnel administrators. Feminists were the first to note that "women's work" was underpaid when compared to "men's work" requiring comparable skills, effort, and responsibility. Several unions recognized this pay inequity and viewed comparable worth policies as an opportunity to benefit their female members and expand their membership. The final actor, government personnel administrators, rarely demanded enactment of equal pay for comparable worth. Instead, they were typically motivated by their own agenda of reforming antiquated classification systems.

These two agendas—reclassification and comparable worth—were often combined into one reform. As separate initiatives, each was doomed: unions opposed reclassification and management opposed comparable worth. But sometimes the two reforms were combined by designing a new classification system that took comparable worth into account. This combination of reforms, however, has tended to undermine the success of comparable worth policies, as I show in chapter 4.

By the late 1970s, the idea of comparable worth received national attention. In 1979 Eleanor Holmes Norton, then chair of the Equal Employment Opportunity Commission, predicted that comparable worth would be "the issue of the 1980s."[12] In 1981 the Supreme Court removed a critical legal barrier to lawsuits over this issue in *County of Washington v. Gunther*. It held that sex discrimination suits filed under Title 7 of the Civil Rights Act were not limited to claims of unequal pay for equal work. Two years later a U.S. district court judge found the state of Washington guilty of intentional discrimination against state employees in jobs dominated by women. The court ordered immediate implementation of the state's comparable worth plan and back pay for employees in jobs held predominantly by women. It was estimated that this ruling would cost the state of Washington hundreds of millions of dollars. Two workers' strikes over this issue also gained national attention, one against the City of San Jose and another against Yale University. In 1984, the Democratic Party endorsed the notion of comparable worth in its party platform.

By the early 1980s, a number of state governments began to implement comparable worth. Minnesota was the first state to enact such legislation and the only state to require local governments to implement comparable worth. Twenty other state governments have also adopted some form of comparable worth pay adjustments. The scope of these policies, however, has varied. The state of New Mexico, for example, spent $3 million in 1983 to increase the salaries of twenty-three female-dominated jobs found in the lowest pay ranges of the state's classification system.[13] The state of Washington, on the other hand, agreed to implement a comparable worth policy costing $115 million that was phased in over a seven-year period ending in 1992.[14]

During the 1980s, opposition to the concept of equal pay for comparable worth grew, especially within the Reagan administration. The president himself denounced the notion as a "cockamamie idea . . . [that] would destroy the basis of free enterprise." The chair of the U.S. Civil Rights Commission referred to it as "the looniest idea since Looney Tunes."[15] Throughout the Reagan and Bush administrations the EEOC rejected any broad interpretation of wage discrimination under Title 7. Other groups have also expressed their opposition to this concept, including members of the business community and the "pro-life" movement.[16]

Although by 1994 this issue appears to have little support in the United States, our neighbor to the north, the Province of Ontario, continues to pursue this policy. In 1987, Ontario passed legislation that requires both public and private sector employers to eliminate pay inequities between predominantly female and male jobs if the jobs are found to be of equal value to the employer. This implementation offers U.S. observers a chance to see how a comparable worth policy might operate if expanded to the private sector. Without U.S. federal government support, however, a large-scale enactment of comparable worth in the United States appears impossible. This is especially true as long as the driving force behind this issue—the women's movement—is busy fighting other battles, most notably over abortion rights.

Where Comparable Worth Policies Have Been Enacted

Hundreds of U.S. state and local jurisdictions have enacted comparable worth measures over the last ten years.[17] Besides the United States, at least two other countries—Australia and Canada—have implemented comparable-worth-type legislation.

U.S. Federal Government. Although the U.S. federal government has never adopted a comparable worth policy, at least three agencies within the executive branch have examined this issue: the Commission on Civil Rights, the Equal Employment Opportunity Commission (EEOC), and the Office of Personnel Management. During the Reagan administration, all three agencies rejected comparable worth as a remedy for sex-based wage discrimination. The Commission on Civil Rights held a consultation on comparable worth in 1984 that examined the usefulness of a comparable worth policy for the United States. The following year, the Commission voted to reject comparable worth as a policy option.[18] That same year, the EEOC decided not to pursue comparable-worth-type wage discrimination cases.[19]

11

The Office of Personnel Management assessed whether the federal work force needed a comparable worth policy and concluded that such a policy was unnecessary.[20]

The Congress has been more supportive of the concept of comparable worth than the executive branch, especially since the Democratic Party regained control of the Senate in 1987. Legislation to conduct a comparable worth study of the federal job classification system passed the House of Representatives several times during the 1980s, but similar bills introduced in the Senate were never formally voted on. At the request of the Congress, the General Accounting Office (GAO) issued several reports that described existing comparable worth policies and outlined federal options for conducting a comparable worth study. In 1989, the GAO began a study of the federal government's pay and classification systems to determine whether gender and/or race bias exists in these systems.

U.S. State Governments. The estimated twenty state governments that have enacted comparable worth policies include California, Connecticut, Hawaii, Illinois, Iowa, Maine, Massachusetts, Michigan, Minnesota, New Jersey, New Mexico, New York, Ohio, Oregon, Pennsylvania, Rhode Island, South Dakota, Vermont, Washington, and Wisconsin.[21] The cost of these policies, however, has varied considerably. Most of these states tended to target a small number of occupations and spent relatively little for comparable worth adjustments. There are several exceptions, however, including California, Connecticut, Iowa, Massachusetts, Michigan, Minnesota, New York, Oregon, Washington, and Wisconsin. Each of these states has spent at least $20 million to implement comparable worth.

U.S. Local Governments. Counties, municipalities, and school districts across the country, from Boston to Los Angeles, have implemented comparable worth policies. The largest concentrations of these enactments, however, are in four states: California, Minnesota, New York, and Washington. One reason these states have witnessed so much activity is that three of the state legislatures—California, Minnesota, and New York—have adopted legislation that, in varying degrees, encouraged local jurisdictions to adopt comparable worth policies.[22] The Minnesota legislature went the farthest in this manner by passing legislation in 1984 that requires all local jurisdictions to undertake comparable worth policies. The state of Minnesota has 855 cities, 435 school districts, and 87 counties, all of whom have undertaken some form of comparable worth policy.[23]

Australia. Australia experienced a dramatic increase in the pay of women relative to that of men during the 1970s. Prior to 1969, the female-to-male pay ratio for full-time workers was relatively constant, around 60 percent. Between 1969 and 1975, this ratio increased 30 percent to a new plateau of 78 percent. Since 1975, women's relative pay in Australia has changed very little.[24] This dramatic increase in women's relative pay was accompanied by three new government policies. Equal pay for equal work was adopted in 1969 and became fully effective three years later. In 1972, the government expanded this policy to equal pay for work of equal value, which was fully implemented by 1975. Finally, in 1974 the government extended the male minimum wage to women.

Despite the apparent success of these government policies for improving women's relative pay, they are not transferable to the United States.[25] Wage determination is highly centralized in Australia, with the government regulating minimum wage levels for almost all occupations. Before 1969, the government maintained separate minimum wages for women and men in each occupation, thus institutionalizing sex discrimination. This policy was reinforced by separate national minimum wages for women and men. The female minimum wage was set at 75 percent of the male minimum. This institutionalized discrimination was eliminated by the three policies discussed above. Since the United States does not have this system of wage determination, these reforms are not applicable here.

Canada. Canada has implemented comparable worth more extensively than any other country in the world. Comparable worth policies have been enacted by the federal government of Canada as well as by seven provincial governments—Manitoba, New Brunswick, Nova Scotia, Ontario, Prince Edward Island, Quebec, and the Yukon.[26] The most far-reaching policy was adopted by Ontario Province in 1987, which requires public sector employers and private sector employers with at least ten employees to implement comparable worth. This legislation is being implemented in stages—the first wage adjustments were given in January 1990 in the public sector. Wage adjustments in the private sector began in January 1991 for employers with at least 500 employees. Smaller firms must implement comparable worth in subsequent years, ending in January 1994, at which time the smallest firms affected by this legislation—those with 10–49 employees—must enact wage adjustments.[27]

The Ontario comparable worth legislation requires both public and private employers to comply with the law, but this law only requires firms to compare female-dominated jobs to a male-dominated job of comparable value. If a male-dominated job of comparable value does not exist within a firm, redress is not necessarily required.[28] For example, suppose a male-dominated job that is valued the same as a nurse within a hospital does not exist. Furthermore, suppose that nurses are found to have 90 percent of the value of pharmacists, but are only paid 80 percent as much as pharmacists. The Ontario law does not require a hospital in this situation to increase nurses' pay to 90 percent of pharmacists' pay. Thus, coverage of the law is restricted. It is estimated that nearly 1.5 million women are covered by the law, but only half of these women will have a comparable male-dominated job.[29] In contrast, state governments in the United States that have enacted comparable worth policies have adopted a broader interpretation of comparable worth that permits proportional comparisons as the one described above.

LEGAL CONTEXT

Ten years ago, many advocates of comparable worth thought that this policy could be advanced through the legal system. In 1981, the U.S. Supreme Court clarified a potential legal barrier to sex-based wage discrimination suits under Title 7. It held in *County of Washington v. Gunther* that sex-based wage discrimination under Title 7 was not limited to instances where women and men performed substantially equal work. At the time, this ruling was seen as opening the door to comparable worth litigation. This door now appears closed due to changes in the composition of the Supreme Court.

Almost thirty years ago, Congress enacted two laws to counteract economic discrimination against women. The first law, the Equal Pay Act (EPA) of 1963, prohibits an employer from paying women and men different wages if they perform equal jobs under similar working conditions within the same establishment. The courts have not required that jobs be identical to be compared under the EPA, but they must be substantially equal. This requirement limits the applicability of the EPA because most men and women work in different jobs. A year later Congress enacted a more comprehensive antidiscrimination law, the Civil Rights Act of 1964, which includes broad-based prohibitions against discrimination. Title 7 of this Act specifically prohibits discrimination in hiring, promotion, termination, and compensation on the basis of race, sex, religion, and national origin.

Title 7 of the Civil Rights Act was linked to the Equal Pay Act through the Bennett Amendment. This amendment permitted an employer to differentiate on the basis of sex in determining wages if such differentiation was "authorized" by the EPA. Prior to 1981, the courts were divided as to what this amendment meant.[30] Some courts held that the Bennett Amendment limited sex-based wage discrimination suits under Title 7 to equal work cases. Others argued that the Bennett Amendment incorporated into Title 7 the four "affirmative defenses" in the EPA that an employer could use to justify sex-based wage differentials. The Supreme Court adopted the latter view in its *Gunther* decision. Thus, according to this ruling, Title 7 can reach sex-based wage discrimination between jobs that are not substantially equal.

The *Gunther* decision, however, left open as many questions as it answered. In particular, the Supreme Court did not clarify the following: (1) what standards of proof could be used in a sex-based wage discrimination suit under Title 7; (2) what types of evidence plaintiffs needed to establish wage discrimination under Title 7; and (3) what defenses an employer could use to justify his/her employment practice. Each of these issues is discussed below.

Standards of Proof. There are two standards of proof that have been used to establish discrimination: disparate treatment and disparate impact. Under the disparate treatment standard, a plaintiff must prove that the employer treated a member of a protected class differently than others because of the person's race, sex, religion, or national origin. Once the plaintiff makes his/her initial or prima facie showing of discrimination, the employer must show that the plaintiff's evidence is false or introduce evidence that the disparate treatment is not caused by intentional discrimination. But the plaintiff always retains the burden of proof in a disparate treatment case, and must show that the employer's defenses are simply a pretext for discrimination.[31]

An example of disparate treatment is an unequal pay for equal work case. In this instance, a member of a protected group is being treated differently since she is paid less than another employee who is performing substantially equal work.

Disparate impact involves the use of a facially neutral employment practice that has a disproportionately adverse impact on members of a protected class. An example of a disparate impact case involves the use of an employment exam, which is a facially neutral employment practice, but which has the adverse effect of disproportionately excluding members of a protected class. Before 1989, it was generally understood that the plaintiff had to show that an employment practice had a disparate impact on a protected group, after which the burden of proof shifted to the employer to show that the employment practice was a business necessity. In 1989, the Supreme Court ruled that once an employment practice was found to have a disparate impact, the employer need only produce some evidence of a "significant business justification" in order to defend the practice.[32] This ruling reversed earlier precedent and found that the burden of proof remained with the plaintiff in disparate impact cases and that the employer only needed to offer some evidence of a significant business justification rather than show that the practice was a business necessity. The Civil Rights Act of 1991 was passed in large part to restore the original interpretation of the disparate impact proof. It states that once the plaintiff shows an employment practice has a disparate impact on a protected group, the employer must show that the "practice is job-related for the position in question and consistent with business necessity."[33]

The *Gunther* case, on the other hand, was a disparate treatment case. The Supreme Court did not rule on whether a disparate impact showing would have been sufficient to establish a prima facie case of sex-based wage discrimination under Title 7. This has been left to the lower courts to decide. Thus far, federal judges have almost uniformly rejected the use of a disparate impact standard in sex-based wage discrimination cases. Some argue that the disparate impact standard is precluded by the fourth defense of the Bennett Amendment, which states that an employer can justify sex-based wage differentials if that difference is due to "any other factor other than sex."[34] One Court of Appeals noted this argument with approval, although it never relied on it to reach a decision.[35] Another argument to preclude the use of the disparate impact standard was used by the Court of Appeals for the Ninth Circuit, which ruled that a specific, clearly delineated employment practice had to be identified in order to use the disparate impact standard.[36]

Evidence Required. Given that the lower courts are limiting sex-based wage discrimination cases to the disparate treatment standard, the next critical issue is the kind of evidence required to establish a prima facie case in a disparate treatment action. In the past, both direct and circumstantial evidence have been used to establish a prima facie case of disparate treatment in employment discrimination cases. The Supreme Court has accepted the view that circumstantial evidence is sufficient to establish a prima facie case of employment discrimination.[37] Nonetheless, almost all of the lower courts have ruled that the kind of circumstantial evidence found in comparable worth studies, namely statistical evidence of unequal pay for comparable jobs, is insufficient to establish a prima facie case of wage discrimination. Some of these courts have ruled that disparate treatment claims must produce direct evidence of discriminatory intent.

Employer Defenses. The final issue that remains unclear regarding sex-based wage discrimination cases is the factors that a defendant can use to justify an employment practice that is found to cause disparate treatment. Thus far, the consensus in the lower courts is that market forces are a legitimate response to allegations of disparate treatment under Title 7. Yet, in 1974 the Supreme Court held that an appeal to market forces could not justify disparate treatment in an equal work case.[38] Despite this Supreme Court ruling, it appears that plaintiffs in Title 7 wage discrimination suits will be required to show that the market forces defense is only a pretext for discrimination.

A review of a well-known comparable worth lawsuit—*American Federation of State, County, and Municipal Employees (AFSCME) v. State of Washington*—illustrates these unresolved issues. In 1983, a federal district court ruled that the state of Washington discriminated on the basis of sex in violation of Title 7 using both the disparate impact and disparate treatment theories. Two years later, this decision was reversed by the Ninth Circuit Court of Appeals, which ruled that the plaintiff could not use the disparate impact theory and that the state's liability under a disparate treatment theory had not been established. This decision was written by Supreme Court Justice Kennedy, who was a member of the Ninth Circuit at the time. Thus,

17

this case shows the views of at least one Supreme Court Justice on this issue.

In 1974, Dan Evans, then governor of Washington State, ordered the first comparable worth study at the request of AFSCME and the State Women's Council.[39] An independent consulting firm was hired to carry out the study, which examined fifty-nine predominantly male and sixty-two predominantly female jobs. The consultant used an a priori factor point job evaluation to rate these jobs. Each job was assigned a point value based on four factors: knowledge and skill, mental demands, accountability, and working conditions. The study found that predominantly female jobs were paid, on average, 20 percent less than predominantly male jobs with equivalent ratings. Governor Evans included a $7 million budget appropriation to begin implementation of comparable worth, but his successor removed the appropriation. Over the next several years, the state legislature continued to examine the issue, but did not fund implementation. In 1981, AFSCME filed a sex-based wage discrimination lawsuit against the state of Washington.

The district court found that the facially neutral employment practice—the state's compensation system—had a disparate impact on employees in predominantly female jobs, as evidenced by the results of the comparable worth study. The court found discriminatory intent was established by direct and statistical evidence, which included the use of want ads that were restricted to a particular sex until 1972 and the testimony of present and former state officials that wages paid to employees in female classes were discriminatory. It added that the state's evidence of paying according to the market was insufficient to justify the disparate impact or disparate treatment.

The Ninth Circuit Court of Appeals reversed this position for the following reasons. First, it ruled that the state's compensation system was not a specific, clearly delineated employment practice, which must be identified in a disparate impact case. It ruled that the state's compensation system was "too multifaceted to be appropriate for disparate impact analysis."[40] Second, it found that the direct evidence presented by the plaintiffs was not persuasive and that the statistical evidence from the comparable worth study was not sufficient to establish disparate treatment. Third, it ruled that the practice of paying prevailing wages was a sufficient defense against a finding of disparate treatment.

With Justice Kennedy on the Supreme Court, a minimum five-vote majority has emerged that will most likely uphold these lower court decisions. Justices Brennan and Marshall, both of whom voted for the *Gunther* decision, have now resigned. Their replacements could vote with other justices to overturn the *Gunther* decision itself. Supreme Court rulings on discrimination cases in 1989 suggest that the Supreme Court will narrowly interpret Title 7. Actions taken by the Court in 1991 further suggest that it is quite willing to overturn Supreme Court precedent. The Civil Rights Act of 1991 codified earlier interpretations of the disparate impact proof, but it is not clear the Supreme Court will allow this standard of proof in sex-based wage discrimination cases brought under Title 7. Advocates of comparable worth will have to use means other than litigation to achieve their goal.

AN OVERVIEW OF THE BOOK

This chapter introduced the concept of comparable worth and provided background information relevant to the policy issue. It also provided a brief review of where comparable worth policies have been enacted and the legal issues involved. State and local governments have taken the lead in this country, with hundreds of jurisdictions adopting comparable worth policies. At the same time, lower court rulings have severely restricted the legal opening left by the Supreme Court in its *Gunther* decision, which held that Title 7 sex-based wage discrimination lawsuits were not limited to equal work cases.

Chapter 2 further defines the concept of the underpayment of "women's work," and reviews the empirical studies that have estimated this underpayment. Almost all of these studies find that female-dominated jobs are paid significantly less than male-dominated jobs even after accounting for productivity-related differences. Many of these studies, however, do not control for the type of industry in which these occupations are found. Hence, new estimates are presented that control for both industry and productivity-related characteristics. This new research finds that "women's work" is paid significantly less than "men's work" even after controlling for industry and productivity attributes. This type of pay inequity explains 20 percent of the total male-female earnings gap.

Chapter 3 reviews the economic explanations for the underpayment of "women's work," which are occupational choice and discrim-

19

ination. Based on this review, I conclude that the underpayment of "women's work" reflects economic discrimination against women. This does not imply intent on the part of employers. It simply means that workers of one sex are being denied economic opportunities available to workers of another sex for reasons unrelated to individual ability. After this description, the chapter presents original research that tests different theories of discrimination. The implications of these findings for Title 7 wage discrimination lawsuits are discussed. Methods are proposed that may overcome some of the objections that the lower courts have had to purely "comparable worth" cases.

Chapter 4 reviews the different procedures used in comparable worth policies and describes the subjective and arbitrary elements of these policies. It summarizes the approaches taken by state governments when implementing comparable worth policies. It proposes policy guidelines to avoid the negative aspects of job evaluation procedures when implementing a comparable worth policy. The estimated costs of enacting comparable worth are reviewed.

Chapter 5 discusses the economic effects of implementing comparable worth policies. It reviews previous empirical estimates of these effects and finds several deficiencies. New empirical findings are presented using data from the state of Minnesota. I find that comparable worth was implemented successfully in this state. It yielded substantial benefits to women working for the state, without producing sizable negative effects on men's earnings or employment opportunities in the state sector.

Chapter 6 summarizes the conclusions of this book. I conclude that a serious problem exists in the U.S. labor market in that women are paid less than men for comparable work. Although comparable worth policies are an imperfect remedy to this problem, they can improve the relative earnings of women without producing serious negative employment effects in the public sector. This suggests that comparable worth could be enacted for federal government employees without significant problems if a gender bias is found. Its extension to the private sector, however, is more problematic. Additional research on the economic consequences of enacting comparable worth in the private sector could inform this debate.

Measuring the Underpayment
of "Women's Work"

T HE PURPOSE of a comparable worth policy is to eliminate the pay
differential between male- and female-dominated jobs that is not explained by productivity-related differences, which I refer to as the
underpayment of "women's work." In general, however, the definition of this concept—the underpayment of "women's work"—has not
been agreed upon. To understand what I mean by the underpayment
of "women's work," I begin by explaining how economists generally
define labor market discrimination. I then relate this definition to the
underpayment of "women's work."

Once I have defined this concept, I review a number of empirical
studies that estimate this pay disparity. These studies are crucial for
understanding the issue of comparable worth because they assess the
need for a comparable worth policy and estimate the potential impact
of this policy on compensation. Most of the existing literature, however, measures the unexplained pay disparity without controlling for
the industry in which the individuals work. In other words, salaries
for child care workers are compared to those of gas station attendants,
for example, even though these workers are found in different industries. Thus, these studies measure a broader concept of pay inequity
than comparable worth policies address. Such policies are designed
to eliminate the underpayment of "women's work" within firms. In
order to estimate the potential impact of comparable worth, national
studies should include detailed industry control variables in their
analysis to control for the type of industry in which the individual
works. Only one empirical study includes industry controls in its
analysis of comparable worth.

Since previous research has not controlled for the type of industry
when analyzing the potential impact of comparable worth, I conclude
this chapter by presenting original empirical research on this subject.
I use data from the 1984 Panel Study of Income Dynamics and the
1983 Current Population Survey to measure the underpayment of
"women's work" after taking into account differences in industry.

MEASURING LABOR MARKET DISCRIMINATION
AGAINST WOMEN

Labor market discrimination is said to exist when two groups of workers are paid differently even though they are equally productive.[1] This form of discrimination can be measured by estimating separate wage equations for women and men and then dividing the pay differential into two parts: (1) that which is due to differences in productivity characteristics; and (2) that which is due to differences in the returns to these characteristics.[2] The latter component is then used as an estimate of discrimination.[3] More specifically, the following equations are estimated:

$$w_i = a + b Z_i \tag{2.1}$$

where i equals either male or female workers; w is a measure of the worker's earnings; Z is a set of productivity-related characteristics; and the a's and b's are the estimated coefficients of the equation.

The gender difference in pay can then be written as:

$$G = \bar{w}_m - \bar{w}_f = b_m (\bar{Z}_m - \bar{Z}_f) + (a_m - a_f) + \bar{Z}_f (b_m - b_f) \tag{2.2}$$

where w_m and w_f are the mean earnings of men and women, respectively; Z_m and Z_f are the mean values of the productivity-related characteristics; and the a's and b's are the estimated coefficients.

The first term measures the portion of the pay gap that is due to differences in mean characteristics between women and men. It is often referred to as the explained component of the pay gap because it can be attributed to differences in characteristics between women and men. The latter two terms measure the extent to which women and men are paid differently for the same characteristics. These terms are typically referred to as the unexplained component because they measure the portion of the pay gap that remains unexplained after differences in characteristics are taken into account. It is also used as a measure of discrimination against women.

The sex pay gap can also be written as:

$$G = \bar{w}_m - \bar{w}_f = b_f (\bar{Z}_m - \bar{Z}_f) + (a_m - a_f) + \bar{Z}_m (b_m - b_f) \tag{2.3}$$

where the variables are defined as above. In this equation, the values multiplied by the first and third components of the sex pay gap, b_f and $\bar{Z}_m$, have been changed. These values are just as valid as the first set, b_m and $\bar{Z}_f$. But the size of these components will differ depending on which set of values is used. This is often referred to as the index problem. Since both are equally valid, analysts often calculate the explained and unexplained components of the sex pay gap both ways and present the average result.

This analysis, however, overlooks the possible earnings loss that results from being employed in a female-dominated job. Occupations are strongly segregated by sex as shown in chapter 1, and it may be that the earnings of women are adversely affected by this segregation. Thus, occupational segregation may contribute to the gender pay disparity.

DEFINING THE UNDERPAYMENT OF "WOMEN'S WORK"

This book defines the underpayment of "women's work" as the earnings loss that an individual suffers if she or he is employed in a job held primarily by women rather than one held primarily by men. One method of estimating the size of the underpayment of "women's work" is to estimate separate earnings equations for women and men that include an explanatory variable that measures the proportion of workers in an occupation who are women, or F, in addition to productivity-related characteristics. I use this approach because it can be used to assess whether employment in a female-dominated job reduces an individual's earnings even after controlling for productivity-related characteristics. The following equation typifies this approach:

$$w_i = a + b\,Z_i + c\,F_i \tag{2.4}$$

where F is a measure of the sex composition of an occupation, and the other variables are defined as in equation (2.1).

A significant coefficient for the variable F indicates that an occupation's gender composition is a statistically important determinant of earnings. If the coefficient c is negative, this implies that individuals earn less if they are employed in a predominantly female occupation rather than a predominantly male one. The size of this pay discrepancy is estimated by the size of c. Since earnings equations are estimated separately for women and men, gender specific measures of the wage penalty are produced, namely c_f and c_m. Both of these estimates are equally valid. Thus, our best estimate of the underpayment is an average of these two coefficients.

23

These estimates can be used to divide the sex pay differential into three parts: (1) that which is due to occupational segregation; (2) that which is due to differences in productivity-related characteristics; and (3) that which is due to differences in estimated coefficients. The portion attributable to the concentration of women in low-paying female-dominated jobs is the following:

$$S_f = c_f (\overline{F}_m - \overline{F}_f) \tag{2.5a}$$

$$S_m = c_m (\overline{F}_m - \overline{F}_f) \tag{2.5b}$$

where $\overline{F}_m - \overline{F}_f$ measures the difference between the men's and women's concentration in female-dominated jobs; and c_f and c_m are the estimated coefficients from the earnings equations.

Since both c_f and c_m are equally valid measures of the wage penalty, S_f and S_m are equally valid measures of the effect of the sex ratio in an occupation on the sex-based earnings gap. Thus, the average of these two calculations is used throughout this discussion.

These earnings equations can be estimated using nationally representative data, such as the Current Population Survey or the 1980 census. Chapter 1 employed this approach using the 1990 Current Population Surveys. The absolute value of the estimated coefficient c was 3.88. Hence, I concluded that women earned $3.88 an hour less if they were employed in an all-female job rather than an all-male one. But this approach measures the underpayment that workers experience while employed in female-dominated jobs, regardless of the industry employing them. In other words, the salaries of child care workers are compared to the salaries of gas station attendants even though they work in different industries. This definition is broader than that addressed by comparable worth policies. Such policies are designed as intra-firm initiatives, eliminating the negative impact of occupational segregation on earnings within firms.

A different approach must be taken to measure the problem addressed by comparable worth policies. One approach is to estimate equation (2.1) for a specific employer. This estimates the negative penalty associated with "women's work" within a single firm. But inferences cannot be made about the extent to which individual earnings, in general, are affected by the underpayment of "women's work." Such inferences can only be made using nationally representative data.

Another approach to estimating the phenomenon that comparable worth policies address is to use national data, but add firm-specific controls to the earnings equations described above. Unfortunately, such variables do not exist in national data sets. Such variables can be approximated, however, with detailed industry control variables that indicate the type of industry employing the individual. Consequently, equation (2.1) becomes:

$$w_i = a + b\,Z_i + c\,F_i + d\,I_i \tag{2.6}$$

where each of the variables has the same definition as before, and I_i is a set of dummy variables that indicate the type of industry employing the individual.

This equation can then be used to estimate the phenomenon that comparable worth policies seek to remedy. The estimated coefficient c measures the pay discrepancy between male- and female-dominated jobs within specific industries after controlling for productivity-related characteristics. The portion of the national sex pay differential explained by the variable F can be calculated in the same manner as equations (2.5a) and (2.5b). A nationwide comparable worth policy would address this part of the national sex pay disparity.

Including industry control variables in the earnings equation is particularly important since women and men are not only segregated by occupation, but also by industry. Furthermore, women tend to be concentrated in low-paying industries, while men are concentrated in high-paying ones. Hence, industrial segregation as well as occupational segregation may contribute to the earnings disparity between women and men. Since comparable worth legislation only addresses the effect of occupational segregation within firms, any negative impact that industrial segregation may have on earnings will be unaffected by such legislation. Consequently, differences in industrial distribution must be controlled for before assessing the potential effect of comparable worth. This restriction means that comparable worth legislation does not eliminate the entire pay disparity between predominantly male and female jobs. It only eliminates the portion that exists within firms.

Measuring the underpayment of "women's work" as described above does not include pay disparities between women and men who work in jobs with similar gender compositions. More specifically, it ignores the fact that men tend to earn more than women within the same occupation. I have imposed this restriction since it reflects the method used by comparable worth policies, which have not examined gender differences within occupations. This approach, however, underestimates the total male-female earnings gap that exists after controlling for productivity differences between women and men. A broader pay equity policy may want to eliminate all of this pay disparity. Nonetheless, this goal goes beyond that of comparable worth as it is currently implemented.

PREVIOUS ESTIMATES OF THE PHENOMENON

This section reviews a new body of empirical literature that emerged in the late 1970s and 1980s that assesses whether workers employed in predominantly female jobs earned less than other workers even after differences in productivity were taken into account. This research uses the definitions of the underpayment of "women's work" described above. Previous reviews of empirical research on the male-female earnings gap were conducted in the early 1980s and did not include this most recent research.[4] Hence, this section offers a comprehensive review of the most recent studies available on the extent to which "women's work" is underpaid.

This review shows that all but one of the studies finds evidence to support the hypothesis that "women's work" is underpaid. Although different methods and data sources are used, these studies consistently found that being employed in a female-dominated job resulted in significantly lower earnings. A summary of these studies is given in table 2.1. The earliest studies estimated the underpayment for the whole economy. These findings, however, are broader than that addressed by a comparable worth policy. Thus, more recent studies estimated firm-specific underpayments or the underpayment after controlling for the industrial composition of the work force. The first set of studies is further divided into three categories according to unit of analysis. The first set of studies uses occupations as the unit of observation, the second uses occupations weighted by the proportion of women or men in each occupation, and the third uses individuals.

Economywide Estimates of the Underpayment

The first two studies, conducted by Snyder and Hudis and Treiman and Hartmann, are very similar.[5] They both use 1970 census data, unweighted occupations as their unit of analysis, and median annual earnings as the dependent variable. The basic difference is that Snyder and Hudis employ more explanatory variables than Treiman and Hartmann. Yet, both of these studies find that annual occupational earnings are significantly affected by the gender composition of the occupation, which is measured by the percentage of women in an occupation, or %F. These studies find that, for women, being employed in an exclusively female occupation rather than an exclusively male one reduces annual earnings by $1,630 to $2,070. Men, on the other hand, experience an even larger pay differential between exclusively female and male occupations, ranging from $2,960 to $3,900 per year.

These studies, which use unweighted occupations as their unit of analysis, test a different hypothesis than the other studies. These studies examine whether occupational segregation reduces *occupational* earnings; the others measure the impact of occupational segregation on *individual* earnings. Unfortunately, these studies can not make inferences about individuals. This limitation is particularly restrictive since we are interested in examining individual outcomes and the impact that employment in a female-dominated job has on relative earnings. In particular, these studies can not determine the extent to which an occupation's sex composition contributes to the male-female earnings gap. Hence, this section of table 2.1 is left blank.

The results of the second set of studies vary considerably despite the fact that these studies use the same unit of analysis, namely occupations weighted by the proportion of women in each occupation. Most notably, the magnitude of the wage penalty declines with each new study. This steady decline is due, in part, to the increasing number of explanatory variables included in each analysis. For example, Ferber and Lowry, and England et al., conducted the first two studies using this analytic design.[6] They found that women earned between $1,438 and $1,682 less per year if they worked in a job that hired women exclusively instead of men. Men under similar circumstances earned between $3,005 and $5,008 less per year. In addition, these authors found that occupational segregation explained between 30 and 42 percent of the national sex pay differential. However, Ferber and Lowry only included two explanatory factors in their analysis— gender composition of the occupation and education. England et al. only included job characteristics, omitting variables that measured individual human capital and demographic characteristics. In contrast, O'Neill and Aldrich and Buchele included a larger array of individual characteristics and different types of job characteristics.[7] O'Neill found that women (men) earned 16 percent (15 percent) less if they were employed in an all-female job rather than an all-male

TABLE 2.1

Summary of Studies Examining Earnings as a Function of an Occupation's Sex Composition

Author and Date of Publication [a]	Data Source	Measure of Earnings	Measure of Sex Composition [c]	Estimated Coefficient for Sex Composition [e]		Percentage of Earnings Gap Explained by Sex Composition [g]			Control Variables [j]
				Female Equation	Male Equation	Female Coeff.	Male Coeff.	Average	

Studies without Detailed Industry Control Variables

Unweighted Occupations as the Unit of Analysis

Snyder and Hudis (1979)	1970 Census	Median Annual	%F	-20.7 (5.6)	-39.0 (7.0)				1,2,7,11,27
Treiman and Hartmann (1981)	1970 Census	Median[b] Annualized	%F	-16.3	-29.6				1

Weighted Occupations as the Unit of Analysis

Ferber and Lowry (1976)	1970 Census	Median Annual	M	1438	5008	19%[h]	66%	42%	1,2
England et al. (1982)	1970 Census	Median Annual for Full-time Workers	F	-1682	-3005	21%	38%	30%	1,26,27,29,30,31,32
O'Neill (1983)	1980 CPS	Log Hourly	F	-.158 (3.24)	-.148 (3.02)	12%	11%	11%	1,2,6,7,11,18,27,28,36,37,38,39
Aldrich and Buchele (1986)	1980 NLS	Hourly	F	-.586	-.686	9%	11%	10%	1,2,4,6,7,12,13,14,26,27,33
Filer (1989)	1980 Census	Hourly for Full-time Workers	F	-.30 (1.25)	.31 (.97)	4%	-4%	0%	1,2,3,9,10,12,13,16,19,28-33,36,39,40-52
England (1992)	1980 Census	Hourly for Full-time Workers	%F	-.004 (2.14)	-.005 (.82)	5%	6%	5%	1,2,12,13,24,26,27,28-33,39,42,45,46,49,56,61,62

Individuals as the Unit of Analysis

U.S. Census (1987)	1984 SIPP	Log Hourly for Full-time Workers	F nhs[d]	-.340 (5.07)	-.241 (4.02)	43%	30%	37%	1,4,5,7,8,9,10,12,13,16-25,34
			hs	-.211 (6.39)	-.225 (8.65)	28%	30%	29%	
			col	-.417 (6.84)	-.189 (3.38)	38%	17%	28%	

Study	Year / Data	Dependent Variable	Measure						References
Blau and Beller (1988)	1981 CPS	Log Annual for White Individuals	DM DB	.156 (15.60) .092 (8.36)	.269 (22.42) .161 (10.73)	12%	21%	17%	1,2,3,6,7,9,10, 13,35,36,53,54
Sorensen (1990a)	1983 CPS	Log Hourly	F	-.201 (8.23)	-.326 (11.67)	20%	33%	27%	1,2,3,5,6,7,8,9, 10,12,13,16,26, 27,28,36
Sorensen (1990a)	1984 PSID	Log Hourly	F	-.248 (7.97)	-.294 (7.43)	25%	29%	27%	1,2,4,5,6,7,8,9, 10,12,13,23,24, 26,27,28,34,60

Studies of Specific Employers

Study	Year / Data	Dependent Variable	Measure						References
Lewis and Emmert (1986)	1981 Federal	Annual for Full-time White Workers	%M	79.29 (28.19)	84.36 (18.97)	35%	37%	36%	1,2,3,5,25,54
Orazem and Mattila (1989)	1983 Iowa	Log Hourly	F	-.258^f (25.80)		59%			1,2,4,5,8,9,12,23, 36,38,54,55,56,57
Killingsworth (1990a)	1981 Minnesota	Log Hourly	F	-.209 (53.41)		43%^{i}			5,8,19,33,38, 54,58,59

Studies With Detailed Industry Control Variables

Study	Year / Data	Dependent Variable	Measure						References
Johnson and Solon (1986)	1978 CPS	Log Hourly	F	-.068 (4.86)	-.160 (10.67)	8%	19%	14%	1,2,3,6,7,8,9, 10,12,13,15,26, 27,28,36,61,62
Sorensen (1990a)	1983 CPS	Log Hourly	F	-.150 (5.75)	-.246 (8.53)	15%	25%	20%	1,2,3,5,6,7,8,9, 10,12,13,15,16,26, 27,28,36
Sorensen (1990a)	1984 PSID	Log Hourly	F	-.227 (6.97)	-.237 (5.98)	23%	24%	23%	1,2,4,5,6,7,8,9, 10,12,13,15,23,24, 26,27,28,34,60

[a] Full citations are given in the references.

[b] Median annualized earnings = (median annual earnings * 2080) mean annual hours.

[c] M = the proportion of workers in an occupation who are men.

%F = the percentage of workers in an occupation who are women.

F = the proportion of workers in an occupation who are women.

DM = a dummy variable that equals one if at least 70% of workers in an occupation are male.

DB = a dummy variable that equals one if the work force in an occupation is between 40% and 70% male.

%M = the percentage of workers in an occupation who are men.

[d] nhs = not a high school graduate.

hs = high school graduate.

col = college graduate.

[e] absolute value of t-statistics are in parentheses when available.

[f] Orazem and Mattila and Killingsworth estimate single earnings equations for both male and female workers, but they include a dummy variable that equals one if the worker is a female and zero otherwise. Thus, they estimate only one coefficient for the sex composition variable. I report this estimated coefficient and calculate the percentage of the earnings gap explained by this variable as described below.

[g] The percentage of the pay gap accounted for by the sex composition of an occupation using the male coefficient was calculated in the following manner:

$$a_m \, (\bar{X}_m - \bar{X}_f) \, / \, (\bar{w}_m - \bar{w}_f)$$

$\bar{X}_m$ and $\bar{X}_f$ are the sample means of the sex composition of an occupation for men and women, respectively. $\bar{w}_m$ and $\bar{w}_f$ are the sample means of the earnings measure for men and women. a_m is the male regression coefficient for the sex composition of an occupation. To derive the figure using the female coefficient, a_m is replaced by a_f.

[h] The gross sex pay differential was not reported in Ferber and Lowry's article. Thus, it was taken from the U.S. Bureau of the Census, *Census of Population: 1970*, Subject Reports, Occupational Characteristics, Final Report PC(2)–7A (Washington, D.C.: GPO, 1973): Table 1. The mean values of M for women and men were also not reported. These were estimated using values from England et al. (1982).

[i] Killingsworth does not report the gender-specific mean values for earnings or the sex composition of the occupation. I have used the following values to calculate the percentage of the earnings gap explained by the sex composition of an occupation. These are derived from my own work using the same original data as Killingsworth, which is from the Minnesota State Personnel Office: X_m = .183, X_f = .765, ln w_m = 2.235, ln w_f = 1.949.

[j] Control variables are: 1. Sex composition of an occuptation. 2. Education. 3. Potential work experience. 4. Actual work experience. 5. Tenure (job and/or employer tenure). 6. Region. 7. Urban. 8. Race. 9. Marital status. 10. Children (number and/or presence). 11. Hours of work. 12. Union status (membership and/or coverage). 13. Government employment. 14. Industry dummies—core/periphery distinctions. 15. Two-digit SIC code industrial categories. 16. Firm size. 17. Involuntarily left last job. 18. Turnover. 19. Health/disability. 20. Blue-collar occupation. 21. High school curriculum. 22. Attended private high school. 23. Obtained advanced degree. 24. Obtained college degree. 25. Various fields of study in college. 26. General Educational Development (from DOT). 27. Specific Vocational Preparation (from DOT). 28. DOT measures of working conditions. 29. DOT measures of cognitive skills. 30. DOT measures of perceptual skills. 31. DOT measures of manual skills. 32. DOT measures of social skills. 33. Race composition of an occupation. 34. Usually work full-time. 35. Part-time last year. 36. Part-time this year. 37. Employed five years earlier. 38. License or certification required. 39. Self-employed. 40. Proportion of workers in an occupation who are noncitizens. 41. Proportion of workers in an occupation who have difficulty with English. 42. Measures of fringe benefits from the Quality of Employment Survey (QES). 43. Proportion of workers in an occupation who have a K401 Plan. 44. Average number of vacation days. 45. Additional measures of effort from the QES, the 1976 Survey of Time Use, and Duncan and Stafford (for a more complete citation see Filer 1989). 46. QES measures of responsibility. 47. QES measures of working conditions. 48. Measures of preferences from Filer and the QES. 49. QES measures of worker's skills. 50. Travel time to work. 51. Professional occupation. 52. Measures of labor market conditions. 53. Inverse Mills' ratio. 54. Veteran status. 55. Professional occupation. 56. Supervisor. 57. Vocational training. 58. Job attributes as measured by a job evaluation. 59. Age. 60. Hometime. 61. Nurturance. 62. Additional Measures of Industrial Characteristics.

one.[8] Aldrich and Buchele found that women (men) earned 59 cents (69 cents) less per hour if they were employed in jobs held exclusively by women rather than men.[9] They both found that occupational segregation explained only 9 to 12 percent of the national sex pay differential.

A more recent study using this analytic design finds that occupational segregation explains none of the national sex-based earnings disparity.[10] Filer finds that although women are paid 30 cents less in an all-female occupation instead of an all-male one, men are paid 31 cents more under similar circumstances. Furthermore, both of these estimated coefficients are insignificant. Thus, Filer concludes that the gender composition of an occupation has no significant impact on earnings. The problem with this study, however, is that it includes so many explanatory variables that it calls into question the interpretation of any one coefficient. Filer includes as many as 225 explanatory factors in his analysis, including such unconventional factors as whether a worker lacks interest in power and the "deadendedness" of a worker's job. Yet, Filer has only 430 observations. Not surprisingly, over half of the estimated coefficients are insignificant. Indeed, many variables that are insignificant in this analysis have been found to have a significant impact on earnings in other studies, including marital status, working part-time, and having difficulty with English. In addition, many of the coefficients that are significant are simply unbelievable. For example, Filer finds that men earn $64 more per hour if they work in a job where everyone goofs off instead of one where no one goofs off.[11]

England undertakes an analysis of the 1980 census that is very similar to Filer's, using many of the same independent variables.[12] England includes an array of variables that measures cognitive, social, and physical skills as well as variables that reflect job amenities, working conditions, and industrial characteristics. All together, she includes seventy-one explanatory factors in her analysis, one-third the number used by Filer. She dropped variables from a larger list to avoid multicollinearity and she dropped variables that generated implausible coefficients, including the variable that measured time spent "goofing off." She found that the sex composition of the occupation explained about 5 percent of the sex pay gap.

The basic problem with this second set of studies is that the unit of analysis, occupations weighted by the proportion of women in the occupation, is an aggregated unit of analysis. Unfortunately, aggregation inevitably results in less efficient estimation and may lead to aggregation bias. The empirical results presented in chapter 1 also suffer from this problem. In contrast, the third set of studies uses individuals as the unit of analysis, a more appropriate analytic design. It permits inferences about individuals without concern regarding possible aggregation bias.

The third set of studies concludes that the gender composition of an occupation has a significant impact on earnings. The Census Bureau finds that women who only complete high school earn 21 percent less in a job held exclusively by women rather than by men.[13] Men earn 23 percent less under similar circumstances. This factor explains 29 percent of the pay gap between women and men who only completed high school. Blau and Beller measure the sex composition of an occupation with two dummy variables.[14] The first equals one if the job is at least 70 percent male; the second equals one if the percent male in the occupation is between 40 and 70. They find that women earn 16 percent more in a job held primarily by men rather than women and 9 percent more if they work in an integrated occupation rather than a female-dominated one. Men earn 27 and 16 percent more under similar circumstances. This study finds that 17 percent of the national sex pay disparity can be attributed to occupational segregation, a smaller figure than that of the U.S. Census.[15] Part of this difference is due to the specification of the sex composition variable. Continuous measures of this variable have a stronger impact on earnings than the dummy variables construct.[16]

Estimates of the Underpayment in Specific Industries

Three other studies have estimated earnings equations with the sex composition of an occupation as an explanatory variable for specific employers. Lewis and Emmert examined male and female earnings in the federal government, Orazem and Mattila examined the earnings structure in the state of Iowa, and Killingsworth examined individual earnings of state workers in Minnesota.[17]

Lewis and Emmert estimated the annual earnings of male and female full-time workers in the federal government as a function of productivity-related characteristics and the percentage of men in an occupation.[18] They found that being employed in an exclusively female occupation rather than an exclusively male one reduces earnings by $7,929 per year for white women and $8,436 for white men.

Furthermore, they found that the sex composition of the occupation explains 35 to 37 percent of the total male-female salary differential in the federal sector.

Using Iowa state payroll data from 1983, Orazem and Mattila estimated a single earnings equation with a dummy variable indicating whether or not the individual was female.[19] This earnings equation also included numerous productivity-related characteristics (listed in table 2.1) as well as the proportion of women in an individual's occupation. They found that earnings are reduced by 26 percent if an individual is employed in an exclusively female occupation rather than an exclusively male one. This factor explains 59 percent of the sex pay disparity in the Iowa state sector.

Killingsworth also estimated a single earnings equation with the following explanatory factors: a gender dummy variable, productivity-related characteristics listed in table 2.1, and the proportion of women in an occupation.[20] He found that being employed in an exclusively female occupation rather than an exclusively male one reduces the earnings of Minnesota state workers by 21 percent, explaining 43 percent of the male-female pay differential in this state sector.

Estimates of the Underpayment within Industries

Johnson and Solon use nationally representative data and an appropriate analytic design for measuring the phenomenon that comparable worth policies seek to eliminate.[21] They not only include the gender composition of an occupation and conventional explanatory factors in their earnings equations, but they also include detailed industry control variables. This study finds that the proportion of women in a worker's occupation has a significantly negative effect on his/her earnings. Women's earnings are reduced by 7 percent if they work in a job held exclusively by women rather than men. Men's earnings are reduced by 16 percent under similar circumstances. The gender composition of an occupation explains 14 percent of the national earnings disparity, the portion that comparable worth legislation seeks to eliminate.

The principal weakness of Johnson and Solon's study is that their data set, the May 1978 Current Population Survey, has limited measures of an individual's education and work experience. Their analytic design is supposed to compare the salaries of individuals working in female-dominated jobs with the salaries of workers in other jobs with similar productivity-related characteristics. Yet, their data cannot adequately measure a key productivity characteristic, actual work experience, and it has no other information about schooling except years completed. Without better measures of human capital, the results of Johnson and Solon should be viewed with caution.

New Empirical Estimates

As the above discussion shows, the existing empirical literature on the extent to which "women's work" is underpaid is somewhat limited. In particular, only a few studies use individuals as the unit of observation when estimating the underpayment of "women's work," the preferred unit of analysis. In addition, most studies omit detailed industry control variables, rendering them silent with regard to the usefulness of a comparable worth policy that is an intrafirm initiative. As a result, new empirical research on this topic is undertaken using data from the 1984 Panel Study of Income Dynamics (PSID) and the May/June 1983 Current Population Survey (CPS). These data were selected in part because they reflected the labor market at the time state governments began to implement comparable worth.

Discussion of the Data

These two surveys, the 1984 PSID and the May/June 1983 CPS, were selected so that comparisons across data sets could be made. The first was selected because it provides detailed information regarding an individual's work experience as well as more conventional demographic and labor market characteristics. This particular CPS was chosen since it includes questions regarding job tenure and firm size in addition to the usual questions concerning employment and demographic status. The PSID consists of all heads of households and wives that are at least 18 years old who reported their hourly earnings. There are 2,619 men in this sample and 2,411 women. The CPS sample refers to all nonagricultural civilian wage and salary workers who are at least 16 years old. There are 9,158 men in this sample and 8,027 women.

The dependent variable in both analyses is the natural logarithm of hourly earnings. The CPS asks the respondents for their usual weekly earnings and usual weekly hours. The logarithm of this ratio is used as the dependent variable. It averages 2.161 for men and 1.731 for women. The ratio of the mean female wage to the mean male wage is .651. In contrast, the PSID asks the respondents for their hourly pay. The logarithm of this value is used as the dependent variable. This variable averages 2.313 for men and 1.891 for women. The ratio of the mean female wage to the mean male wage is .655.

The independent variable measuring the proportion of women in an occupation, called F, is constructed from the 20 percent sample of the 1980 U.S. census.[22] There are 503 three-digit level occupational categories in this data set. This data is particularly well suited for constructing this variable since it is such a large data set (about 20 million people), averaging over 40,000 individuals in each occupation.

Job attributes are also included as independent variables in this analysis. They were derived from the fourth edition of the *Dictionary of Occupational Titles*.[23] Five variables are included which describe the following characteristics of an occupation: the general educational requirement, the specific vocational preparation requirement, the strength requirement, the physical demands, and the undesirable environmental conditions associated with a job. These variables are included in the analysis because it is anticipated that these job characteristics are rewarded but are not adequately captured by other explanatory variables.

The other independent variables are taken from the PSID or the CPS, respectively. These are conventional variables included in most earnings equations, as evidenced by their similarity to control variables listed in table 2.1. Although most of the explanatory variables are the same in both the PSID and CPS data sets, there are three major differences. First, the PSID data includes more measures of human capital than the CPS data. In addition to education and tenure, it includes actual work experience, whether an individual has obtained a B.A. degree or an advanced degree, and time spent out of the labor force, which the CPS does not have.[24] In the CPS analysis, actual work experience is proxied by potential work experience, defined as age minus education minus six. Furthermore, the measures of part-time work differ in these data sets. The CPS asks individuals whether they are currently working part-time voluntarily or involuntarily. These questions are not asked by the PSID. Instead, they ask respondents how many hours they worked last year. If they said they worked more than 1,820 hours (i.e., more than 35 hours a week for 52 weeks), then this individual is coded as a full-time worker last year. Finally, the CPS includes information about the size of the firm employing the respondent, but the PSID does not.

Empirical Findings

The underpayment of "women's work" is estimated with and without detailed industry dummy variables. The earnings equations without detailed industry control variables include a wide array of explanatory variables thought to influence earnings (for a complete list see table 2.1). These equations are similar to those estimated by the U.S. Census Bureau and Blau and Beller.[25] Such variables as region, SMSA size, union status, government employment, and five variables measuring job characteristics are also included in this analysis. The equations using PSID data, however, include a more comprehensive set of human capital variables than the equations using the CPS.

The earnings equations with detailed industry dummy variables include all of the variables described above as well as forty-two industry dummy variables. These estimates take industrial differences into account before estimating the underpayment of "women's work." Thus, they yield a more appropriate estimate of the phenomenon that comparable worth policies seek to eliminate, since such policies are designed as intrafirm initiatives.

A summary of the regression results is included in table 2.1. This table shows that workers in female-dominated jobs earn significantly less than other workers regardless of the data set used or the specification of the earnings equation. The size of the estimated coefficient for the variable F declines once the detailed industry control variables are added to the earnings equation, but the coefficient remains significant. In the earnings equations without industry controls, women earn 20 to 25 percent less in an all-female job rather than an-all male one. Men earn 29 to 33 percent less under similar circumstances. Once detailed industry control variables are added to the earnings equations, the wage penalty associated with "women's work" declines somewhat. In this model, women earn 15 to 23 percent less in an exclusively female occupation rather than an exclusively male one. Men earn 24 to 25 percent less in similar circumstances.

Table 2.1 also shows that the variable F explains a substantial portion of the national sex pay differential. Using the earnings equations without detailed industry controls, the sex composition of an occupation explains 27 percent of the national sex pay gap. Once industrial distribution is taken into account, the sex composition of an occupation explains 20 to 23 percent. This is the portion of the national pay disparity that comparable worth legislation seeks to eliminate. Thus, this research finds that national comparable worth legislation would address a sizable component of the national sex pay differential. If this policy is implemented on a smaller scale, of course, its ability to remedy these national earnings discrepancies would be reduced.

The results from the first model of earnings are similar to previous research using individuals as the unit of analysis, which found that 17 to 37 percent of the national sex pay disparity can be attributed to occupational segregation.[26] In contrast, these findings are quite different from the results of more recent studies using weighted occupations as the unit of analysis, which found that occupational segregation explained less than 12 percent of the national sex pay differential.[27]

The conclusions drawn from the earnings equation with detailed industry control variables contrast with those of Johnson and Solon, the only authors using the same analytic design.[28] Research presented here finds a sizable pay disparity between male- and female-dominated jobs using this model. Johnson and Solon, on the other hand, use the same analytic design but find a much smaller pay disparity between male- and female-dominated jobs. Moreover, they conclude that after controlling for industrial segregation, occupational segregation explains only 14 percent of the national sex pay differential. In contrast, this research finds that 20 to 23 percent of the male-female earnings gap is due to the gender composition of the occupation.

These different findings are not entirely surprising since the analyses use different years of data and different explanatory factors. Johnson and Solon use 1978 CPS data; this analysis uses data from 1983 (CPS) and 1984 (PSID). Other research suggests that the impact of the sex composition of an occupation on earnings has increased during the 1970s and early 1980s.[29] In addition, Johnson and Solon use two variables not included here: the proportion of individuals in an occupation who are working part-time and the proportion of individuals in an occupation who are covered by a union contract. It is quite likely that these variables are correlated with the proportion of women in an occupation. If they are, their presence in an earnings equation will reduce the significance of the variable F. In contrast, the CPS equations in this study include two variables not included in Johnson and Solon's analysis, tenure and firm size. These variables, however, are not particularly correlated with the proportion of women in an occupation.[30]

Other Results from the Earnings Model with Industry Controls

It has been argued that once differences in industrial distribution between women and men are taken into account, the effect of occupational segregation on earnings is minimal. For example, Johnson and Solon state, "The most important implication of these results is that, since CW [comparable worth] would not apply across industries . . . , it is unlikely to eliminate a major fraction of the disparity between women's and men's wages."[31] To examine this issue, table 2.2 reports the percent of the male/female earnings gap that is explained by different groups of explanatory factors.

Table 2.2 shows that occupational segregation accounts for 20 to 23 percent of the sex-based earnings differential. At the same time, industrial segregation explains 12 to 17 percent of the earnings disparity. Thus, although industrial segregation contributes to the earnings disparity between women and men, this analysis finds that occupational segregation plays a more significant role.

Once occupational and industrial segregation are controlled for, table 2.2 shows that differences in education and experience account for very little of the earnings gap (only 7 percent) when CPS data are used, but they account for one-fourth of the gap when using PSID data. As discussed earlier, the PSID data have much richer measures of human capital than the CPS. Therefore, it does not come as a great surprise that the analysis using PSID data finds considerably more of the male-female pay gap is due to sex-based differences in human capital variables. This points out the severe limitations of the measures of human capital in the CPS.

Table 2.2 also shows that between 22 and 43 percent of the national sex pay disparity is left unexplained by differences in explanatory variables. As I explained earlier, analysts have often referred to this figure as a measure of wage discrimination.[32] Yet, most of this earlier

TABLE 2.2

Percent of Sex Pay Disparity Accounted for by Different Factors

	PSID DATA	CPS DATA
Total Sex Pay Gap (in dollars)	$3.49	$3.03
Occupational Segregation	23%	20%
Industrial Differences	17%	12%
Differences in Education and Work Experience[a]	25%	7%
Differences in Other Factors[b]	12%	18%
Unexplained Residual	22%	43%

Sources: Current Population Survey (CPS), May/June 1983; Panel Study of Income Dynamics (PSID), 1984; U.S. Census, 1980 (1983); Dictionary of Occupational Titles (DOT), as reported in Miller et al. 1980.

[a] Variables included in education and work experience are: education (both data sets), B.A. degree (PSID), advanced degree (PSID), potential work experience (CPS), actual work experience (PSID), tenure (both), and hometime (PSID).

[b] Variables included with other factors are: geographical region, urban, race, marital status, children, part-time, union status, government employment, and DOT variables.

research included only productivity-related characteristics in their analysis, not occupational segregation and industry control variables as this analysis has done.[33] In these studies, the unexplained component measured that portion of the national sex pay differential which was unexplained by differences in productivity between women and men. Indeed, this was their definition of wage discrimination. In contrast, this analysis measures the effect of occupational segregation on earnings. The unexplained component in this analysis only captures that portion of the sex pay disparity which remains after taking into account occupational segregation as well as differences in productivity-related characteristics between women and men. Not surprisingly, this analysis finds smaller unexplained residuals than most earlier research.

SUMMARY

All but one of the studies reviewed here finds that being employed in a female-dominated job reduces one's earnings. However, the magnitude of this underpayment varies considerably, accounting for anywhere between zero and 42 percent of the pay differential between women and men. In addition, existing empirical research is hindered by two fundamental drawbacks. First, most studies use occupations rather than individuals as their unit of analysis. Unfortunately, this aggregation results in less efficient estimation and possible aggregation bias, without any apparent gain. Second, most of the studies omit detailed industry control variables. Thus, the effect of occupational segregation and the impact of the differing industrial distributions of women and men on earnings cannot be separated. Separating these effects is particularly important when estimating the size of the phenomenon that comparable worth policies remedy, since these policies are intrafirm initiatives. The only study that overcomes both of these fundamental drawbacks uses a data set that has only weak measures of human capital variables.

Original research was conducted to overcome the weaknesses in the existing literature. Results show that being employed in a female-dominated job significantly reduces individual earnings, suggesting that an underpayment for "women's work" does exist. This factor explains approximately 27 percent of the sex-based pay gap. When this phenomenon is measured within industries, this research shows that an underpayment still exists for female-dominated jobs, explaining about one-fifth of the sex-based earnings disparity. This latter estimate is a more appropriate measure of the phenomenon that comparable worth legislation seeks to eliminate, suggesting that this policy seeks to remedy a sizable component of the male-female earnings gap.

Is the Underpayment of "Women's Work" Discrimination?

T WO FINDINGS—occupational segregation by sex and the wage penalty associated with female-dominated jobs—need to be explained. Economic theory offers two explanations for these phenomena. The first, occupational choice, holds that women and men make different choices with regard to their labor market involvement and these choices result in occupational segregation and lower relative earnings for women. Two theories of occupational choice are reviewed below—the human capital model and the theory of compensating differentials. These theories, however, can not explain why workers in female-dominated jobs are paid less than other workers after controlling for productivity differences. Instead, adherents of these explanations argue that the wage penalty associated with "women's work" is due to misspecification of the earnings equation. I show that efforts have been made to correct for misspecification, yet research still finds that workers in predominantly female jobs earn less than workers in other jobs even after controlling for productivity differences.

The second explanation for occupational segregation and lower pay for "women's work" is that women are discriminated against in the labor market. Two theories of discrimination are reviewed—the crowding hypothesis and the institutional theory of labor market discrimination. I present new empirical research that assesses the relevance of these two theories for explaining the underpayment of "women's work." I find that the crowding hypothesis is the best explanation for the wage discrepancy between male- and female-dominated jobs in the private sector, but the institutional model of discrimination more accurately explains this phenomenon in the public sector.

Legal and policy implications of this research are discussed. The first implication of this research is that the market salaries of female-dominated jobs reflect employment discrimination against women. But, this kind of discrimination is not prohibited under Title 7 of the

Civil Rights Act according to several appellate court opinions. Second, the average private sector employer does not pay female-dominated jobs significantly less than male-dominated jobs once productivity characteristics and market forces are taken into account. This suggests that if the Supreme Court upholds the general consensus among the appellate courts regarding sex-based wage discrimination cases, these lawsuits will have little effect on women's salaries. On the other hand, in the public sector I find that the sex composition of an occupation is a significant factor in wage determination even after controlling for productivity characteristics and market forces. Hence, Title 7 lawsuits could succeed in the public sector, but plaintiffs must show that disparate treatment exists even after controlling for market forces. I offer a methodology for this purpose.

It is important to note that different disciplines define discrimination in different ways. Economists generally define discrimination as the pay difference between two groups of workers that is not accounted for by productivity differences.[1] This is not a legal definition of discrimination, but rather an economic one, developed and used by economists to determine the extent to which individuals in one social category are denied economic opportunities available to other individuals of another social category for reasons that have little or nothing to do with their individual abilities. This kind of discrimination does not imply intent on the part of employers. As I showed in chapter 2, economic discrimination can be further divided into several types, one of which exists when an employer pays workers in one sex-typed occupation less than workers in another sex-typed occupation even though the two groups of workers are performing work that requires comparable skills, effort, responsibility, and working conditions. This is the kind of discrimination that comparable worth policies seek to remedy.

OCCUPATIONAL CHOICE MODELS

Two economic theories of occupational choice have been developed, one that relies on the human capital model and the other based on the theory of compensating differentials. Both occupational choice models are based on assumptions of voluntary occupational choice. The first one, the human capital model, is based on the voluntary choices that women and men make with regard to their involvement in the labor market. Human capital theory states that individuals make decisions regarding education and training on the basis of perceived costs and expected benefits associated with each. Furthermore, it is noted that a sexual division of labor exists within most families, where women take responsibility for maintenance of the home and raising the children and men provide the financial support. It is argued that because of this division of labor, women anticipate shorter and more discontinuous involvement in the labor market than men. This reduces their long-run payoff to human capital investments since they expect fewer years in the work force over which to reap the returns. Thus, women will choose jobs that do not require large investments in human capital. In particular, women will avoid jobs that require long periods of specific or vocational training. Furthermore, they will choose jobs that do not impose a large wage penalty for intermittent employment. These will be occupations that require little human capital investment or human capital that does not atrophy with disuse. These occupations will be low paying since their human capital requirements are low. Consequently, the human capital model predicts occupational segregation by sex and relatively low earnings for women.

The second occupational choice model used to explain occupational segregation and low relative earnings for women is referred to as the theory of compensating differentials and heterogeneous preferences. This theory states that nonwage characteristics of jobs may give rise to compensating wage differentials if workers find these characteristics unattractive and employers find it difficult to hire workers in these jobs. Furthermore, they argue that women and men have different preferences regarding job amenities. According to this view, men place a greater emphasis on earnings and less on amenities, while women do just the opposite. This model predicts that women will tend to select occupations that are relatively low paying but have certain job attributes, such as good working conditions, flexible work schedules, and little overtime. Men, on the other hand, will tend to select occupations that are relatively high paying but do not offer such amenities. This dichotomy arises because of the sexual division of labor in the home, where women are primarily responsible for household maintenance and child care and men are the primary breadwinners.

Both the human capital model and the theory of compensating differentials predict occupational segregation and lower relative earn-

ings for women. However, neither model predicts that the sex composition of an occupation will affect earnings if the regression model of
earnings is properly specified. Adherents to these models claim that
a significant coefficient for the sex composition variable results from
misspecification of the model. The most frequently cited misspecification in these analyses is that insufficient measures of human capital
characteristics or job amenities are included in the regression model
of earnings. For example, many of these studies do not include measures of time spent out of the labor force or time taken to train for
jobs, two measures emphasized by the human capital theory of occupational choice. Similarly, adherents to the compensating differential
theory of occupational choice argue that analyses of earnings should
include variables that reflect such factors as unfavorable working conditions on a job, availability of flexible scheduling, and commuting
time to work. If these types of variables are not included in the analysis, the coefficient for the sex composition variable will be biased
since it is probably correlated with the omitted variables. Thus, according to proponents of this theory, the negative wage penalty associated with female-dominated jobs is not a measure of discrimination,
but a measure of the bias due to omitted variables in the earnings
equation.

There are a number of problems with this argument. First, empirical research presented in the last chapter, in table 2.1, certainly
included a large array of human capital characteristics of the individual and occupation. Nonetheless, most of these studies find significant and substantial wage penalties associated with employment
in female-dominated jobs. Thus, serious efforts have been made to
incorporate measures of human capital into these analyses, yet the
sex composition variable is still a major factor contributing to lower
earnings. Furthermore, although most empirical work on this subject has not included measures of job characteristics, my own work
included five such measures: general educational development, specific vocational preparation, bad working conditions, strength requirements, and physical demand requirements. Of course, this is
not an exhaustive list of job attributes, and future research on this
topic should include more of these variables. However, it does mean
that some of the negative job attributes that workers, especially
women, are expected to avoid have been incorporated into this analysis. Yet this work still finds sizable negative coefficients for "women's
work."

Furthermore, previous research provides only limited support for the theory of compensating differentials. This model predicts that workers make trade-offs between job attributes and income. Thus, according to this model, jobs with positive attributes, such as flexible scheduling, should pay lower salaries than jobs without these attributes. Similarly, negative job attributes, such as bad working conditions and strength requirements, should increase salaries. Empirical studies of this subject, however, have often found wrong-signed or insignificant estimates of these wage differentials.[2]

Three extensions of this empirical research have been conducted that attempt to reduce the impact of unobserved productivity differences among individuals.[3] All three efforts, however, have found that "women's work" is still underpaid despite a more sophisticated econometric model. The first study corrected for possible selection bias due to the decision whether or not to work before estimating earnings equations like those described in chapter 2.[4] Previous research on the pay differential between "women's work" and "men's work" had overlooked the issue of self-selection into the labor market. This oversight, however, could lead to biased estimates of the coefficients in the earnings equations. To overcome this weakness, Blau and Beller employed a Heckman-selection technique to obtain consistent estimates of the coefficients in their earnings equations. They found that even after correcting for possible selection bias and controlling for productivity differences, women who worked in male-dominated jobs earned 16 percent more than women who worked in female-dominated jobs.

The second study, conducted by England et al., estimated a fixed-effects model to estimate the pay disparity between male- and female-dominated jobs.[5] The central notion of this model is to estimate differences in pay between predominantly male and female jobs for the same worker overtime. Using this approach, England et al. found that women earned significantly less when employed in female-dominated jobs rather than male-dominated ones.[6]

A third approach for reducing the impact of omitted variables is to estimate a bivariate selectivity model, where the individual's decision to work and occupational choice are explicitly modeled. If the decision to work and the decision to select a female-dominated job are explicitly modeled as choice variables, then the earnings equations can be corrected for possible selection bias caused by both sources of self-selection. I conducted such an analysis and found that women in female-dominated jobs earned 6 to 15 percent less than women in other occupations even after controlling for these two sources of possible selection bias.[7]

Hence, empirical studies have repeatedly found sizable pay disparities between male- and female-dominated jobs even after controlling for productivity differences. The large number of studies weighs against adherents of the occupational choice model who claim this pay disparity only reflects model misspecification and not discrimination.

DISCRIMINATION THEORIES

There are two theories of discrimination which posit that employer discrimination results in occupational segregation and wage penalties for female-dominated jobs: the institutional model and the crowding model.[8]

Institutional Model of Discrimination

The institutional model states that certain firms develop internal labor markets.[9] Within these markets the determination of wages and the allocation of workers are governed by a set of rules and customs rather than direct supply and demand. Management adopts an internal labor market if they want to decrease worker turnover, recoup investments in firm-specific training, and increase organizational loyalty. Employees prefer this arrangement because it offers increased job security, promotional opportunities, and a sense of fair play.

According to the institutional model of discrimination, firms with internal labor markets are more likely to discriminate than other firms. Since they use occupations rather than individuals as their unit of decision to establish pay and promotional opportunities, individuals within these occupations are treated similarly. Hence, it is to the firm's advantage to make sure that workers within each job are as similar as possible. Societal norms and prejudices influence management's view regarding which characteristics are relevant when making job assignments. The social order within the larger community has established separate roles for women and men and has ranked "women's work" less valuable than that of "men's work." Firms with internal labor markets incorporate and reinforce these norms by using gender to assign individuals different occupations. They also pay "women's work" less than they would if it were performed by men, simply because "women's work" is less valued by society. Thus, internal labor markets reflect and reproduce societal discrimination against women, and result in a more segregated work force with lower salaries for "women's work" than would exist without internal labor markets.

According to institutional labor economists, certain sectors of the economy are more likely than others to adopt internal labor markets, including public sector employers, large firms, unionized firms, capital-intensive firms, and firms that operate in concentrated product markets.[10] Public sector labor relations tend to be highly structured, characterized by rigid wage schedules, extensive job classification systems, and detailed job ladders. Within the private sector, firms that employ large numbers of individuals tend to establish internal labor markets more than other firms. Greater numbers encourage rationalization of personnel functions and the implementation of internal labor markets. Similarly, firms that are unionized tend to adopt internal labor markets because unions frequently demand job security and fairness. Industries in which a few large firms dominate the product market are more likely than other industries to develop internal labor markets. Concentrated product markets yield higher levels of profits due to the lack of competition. These higher profits may be used to rationalize firms' personnel function and decrease labor turnover.

Crowding Hypothesis

The crowding hypothesis, another model of discrimination, posits that labor market discrimination results in occupational segregation and a wage penalty for "women's work." It states that employers discriminate against women by excluding them from occupations considered to be "men's work."[11] Since these jobs are reserved for men, relatively few women are hired into these positions. Given that the demand for women in these jobs is limited, they are crowded into other occupations, typically referred to as "women's work." The supply of women accordingly increases for "women's work," which in turn reduces their wage. For simplification, this model assumes that women and men have equal abilities and without discrimination would be paid equally. Consequently, it predicts that because of discrimination women and men are segregated into different occupations and that those doing "women's work" earn less than those doing "men's work," even though all workers are equally well qualified for both occupations.

Both models of discrimination, the institutional and crowding theories, assert that employer discrimination leads to occupational segregation and lower earnings for "women's work." Yet, the processes that produce these results are quite different. The crowding model posits that employers restrict women's employment opportunities, which results in the overcrowding of women into female-dominated jobs. This excess supply of workers depresses the market wages for "women's work." Thus, all employers, whether they discriminate or not, will pay lower salaries to female-dominated jobs, since the market wage has been depressed. In contrast, the institutional model claims that firms that adopt internal labor markets are more likely than other firms to segregate their work force and pay salaries that reflect the "femaleness" of the occupation. These practices are due to the incorporation of societal prejudices against women into the rules and customs governing the internal labor market. According to this theory, firms that do not adopt internal labor markets pay the market wage.

Empirical Tests of Alternative Discrimination Theories

To test the institutional model of discrimination, I compare the wage structure of employers who are expected to have an internal labor market with the wage structure of those who are not expected to have an internal labor market. I first examine large and small firms, followed by core and periphery firms. Both analyses use the Current Population Survey from May/June 1983.

Since this model predicts that large firms are more likely than small firms to adopt an internal labor market, this model expects the wage penalty associated with female-dominated jobs to be greater in large firms. This hypothesis can be tested using CPS data, since this particular survey asked respondents about the size of their firm. The CPS data for private sector workers was divided into two sets depending on the size of the firm employing the individual. An individual is said to work for a small firm if the individual works with fewer than 25 employees. If the individual works with more than 25 employees, she or he is said to work for a large firm. Separate earnings equations for women and men were estimated for each of these divisions. Table 3.1 summarizes these results.

Table 3.1 shows inconsistent evidence for the institutional model of discrimination. For men, it shows that the wage penalty associated with employment in a female-dominated job is greater in large firms than in small firms, thus supporting the institutional model of discrimination. The estimated coefficient for the variable F decreased from $-.130$ in small firms to $-.227$ in large firms. This means that men employed in all-female jobs rather than all-male jobs earned 13 percent less if they were employed in a small firm and 23 percent less if they were employed in a large firm. However, results are the opposite for women. Women who worked for small firms received a greater wage penalty for employment in a female-dominated job than women who worked in large firms. In small firms, women earned 24 percent less if they were employed in an all-female job rather than an all-male one. But, in large firms, the wage differential between all-female and all-male jobs was only 11 percent. Thus, these results contradict the institutional model. Taking the average of the male and female coefficients, I find that the average effect of being employed in a female-dominated job is not substantially different in small and large firms.

Some adherents to the institutional model divide industries into two sectors, referred to as the core and periphery.[12] Core industries are capital intensive with high unionization and profit rates. Periphery industries are labor intensive, have little unionization, and low profit rates. It is expected that core industries are more likely to adopt internal labor markets than periphery industries. Thus, this model of discrimination predicts that the wage penalty for female-dominated jobs should be larger among core sector industries. To test this hypothesis, I divided the CPS data for private sector workers according to the type of industry employing the individual. Using the categorization of industries into core and periphery sectors developed by Beck, Horan, and Tolbert, I estimated separate earnings regressions for women and men within each industrial sector.[13] The results of these regressions are also summarized in table 3.1.

Table 3.1 shows that the wage penalty associated with female-dominated jobs is larger in the periphery sector than in the core sector for both women and men. For women, the wage penalty associated

TABLE 3.1

Summary of Regression Results by Firm Size and Industrial Sector

	Estimated Coefficient for the Variable F		
	Female equation	Male equation	Average
Small Firms	−.240 (4.46)	−.130 (2.17)	−.185
Large Firms	−.110 (2.92)	−.227 (5.59)	−.169
Periphery Sector	−.365 (6.65)	−.329 (6.13)	−.347
Core Sector	−.067 (1.72)	−.075 (1.67)	−.071

Sources: Private sector workers from Current Population Survey (May/June 1983); U.S. Census, 1980 (1983); and the DOT, as reported by Miller et al. 1980.
Note: Absolute value of t-statistics in parentheses.

with female-dominated jobs is 37 percent in the periphery sector but only 7 percent among core sector industries. Similarly, for men, the wage penalty is 33 percent in the periphery and 8 percent in the core. These results also contradict the institutional theory of discrimination.

To test the crowding hypothesis, I added another explanatory variable to the basic earnings equations used in table 3.1. This variable is the average female wage in an occupation as reported by the 1980 U.S. census. The crowding model predicts that discrimination reduces the market wage for "women's work." This variable can be proxied by the average female occupational wage. Thus, according to the crowding model, once women's occupational wage is taken into account, being employed in a female-dominated job will no longer reduce earnings. On the other hand, the institutional model of discrimination would expect the variable F to remain significant even after the market wage proxy has been included in the analysis, since most of the work force is covered by internal labor markets which presumably use the sex composition of an occupation to determine wages.

The voluntary choice models, on the other hand, would not expect the variable proxying market wages to have an independent effect on

TABLE 3.2

Summary of Regressions That Include the Female Occupational Wage as an
Explanatory Variable

	Estimated Coefficients for the Variable F			
	PSID DATA		CPS DATA	
	female equation	male equation	female equation	male equation
Private Sector				
w/o occupational wage	−.230 (5.41)	−.110 (2.27)	−.167 (5.34)	−.196 (5.76)
with occupational wage	−.032 (.69)	−.043 (.83)	−.035 (1.05)	−.077 (2.14)
Public Sector				
w/o occupational wage	−.224 (4.15)	−.471 (6.24)	−.206 (4.10)	−.340 (5.73)
with occupational wage	−.0004 (.01)	−.385 (4.77)	−.118 (2.132)	−.319 (5.01)

Sources: Panel Study of Income Dynamics (1984); Current Population Survey (May/June 1983); U.S. Census, 1980; (1983); and DOT as reported by Miller et al. 1980.

Note: Absolute value of *t*-statistics in parentheses.

earnings. According to these models, if the earnings equations were properly specified, neither the variable F nor the market wage proxy would influence earnings. Thus, their significance is assumed to exist only because these variables are correlated with productivity or supply factors that have not been included in the analysis.

Table 3.2 summarizes the regression results after the female occupational wage is added to the earnings equations as an explanatory variable. It shows that in the private sector the wage penalty associated with female-dominated jobs declines dramatically once the occupational wage for women is included in the earnings equation. Before its inclusion, workers earn between 11 and 23 percent less if they work in an all-female job rather than an all-male one. After its inclusion, the wage penalty drops to less than 8 percent. Furthermore, in three out of four of the estimated equations, this coefficient is not significantly different from zero. This strongly suggests that in the private sector discrimination operates according to the crowding model, with employment discrimination reducing the market wage for female-dominated jobs.

Table 3.2 also summarizes the results for the government sector. In this sector of the economy, the estimated coefficient for F declines somewhat after adding the female occupational wage as an explanatory variable. Before the inclusion of the female occupational wage, the results show that all-female jobs earn between 21 and 47 percent less than all-male jobs. After this variable is included in the analysis, this wage penalty ranges from 0 to 39 percent. Nonetheless, in three out of four of these equations, the estimated coefficient for F is still significantly different from zero. This suggests that in the public sector, the institutional model of discrimination, rather than the crowding theory, explains the negative relationship between the "femaleness" of an occupation and earnings.

Hence, I find evidence in support of the crowding model in the private sector, but the institutional model provides a better explanation of discrimination in the public sector. It could be argued that these results show private sector employers are not discriminating against women, they are simply paying market wages. But this relies on a narrow definition of discrimination. It says that an employer may not have exclusionary practices, but she or he can take advantage of a discriminatory outcome, namely lower wages in "women's work," which only exists because of discrimination. On the other hand, if you rely on an economic definition of discrimination, private sector employers are discriminating against women because they pay different salaries to men and women that are not accounted for by productivity differences. Therefore, I conclude that these employers are discriminating against women.

Legal and Policy Implications

These empirical results suggest several points regarding Title 7 sex-based wage discrimination lawsuits. First, if market forces are permitted as a legal defense against disparate treatment, it will be harder for plaintiffs to establish discrimination against private sector employers. Several appellate courts have ruled that employers may use market forces as a legal defense against disparate treatment in sex-based wage discrimination lawsuits. Such a ruling, if upheld by the Supreme Court, could mean that relatively few lawsuits will succeed against private sector employers. This research shows that once productivity-related characteristics and prevailing wages are taken into account, the average private sector employer does not pay workers in predominantly female jobs significantly less than those in predominantly male jobs. In other words, pay disparities found between comparable male- and female-dominated jobs in the private sector are, on average, driven by market forces. Of course, there may be isolated cases where a private sector employer is not paying prevailing wages.

On the other hand, this research shows that the average public sector employer does pay female-dominated jobs less than male-dominated jobs even after controlling for market forces and productivity differences. Hence, sex-based wage discrimination lawsuits should be more successful in the public sector. Of course, plaintiffs will still need to establish a prima facie case of disparate treatment with direct as well as statistical evidence according to the appellate courts that have ruled on this issue. But, most plaintiffs in these initial cases have had direct and statistical evidence of disparate treatment. Nonetheless, they have not been able to refute an employer's assertion that the pay disparities reflect market forces.

The regression methods used in this chapter can be used by plaintiffs to show that market forces cannot explain the pay disparity between female- and male-dominated jobs. The first step of this process is to determine the prevailing wages for most jobs in the firm. This kind of information may be available from the employer through court discovery proceedings. Many employers have conducted salary surveys of other firms. If the firm does not have this kind of information, the plaintiff can hire an independent consultant to survey other firms. In either case, this information can be added as an independent variable in the salary equations that are estimated in comparable worth studies. Better yet, the plaintiff can estimate earnings equations for individuals in the firm as I have done here for the U.S. economy. These individual earnings equations are more relevant in Title 7 lawsuits, since the plaintiff is trying to establish that members of a protected class are being discriminated against, not that female-dominated jobs are paid less than male-dominated jobs. If these regression results show that wages are still significantly affected by the sex composition of an occupation even after accounting for market forces and productivity differences, this may be used by the plaintiff to show that the employer is using market forces as a pretext for discrimination.

Finally, these results show that women working in female-dominated jobs experience economic discrimination, but the current interpretation of Title 7 by several appellate courts does not prohibit this kind of discrimination. The only kind of sex-based wage discrimination that currently appears to be prohibited by Title 7 is when an employer is shown to have intentionally discriminated against women in female-dominated jobs and to have done so for illegitimate reasons, not simply because the employer followed market forces. This prohibition of discrimination is so narrowly defined that very few women will find relief under these terms. Broad relief of wage discrimination against women will require further legislation.

Summary

Economic theory provides two explanations for occupational segregation and relatively low earnings for women—different voluntary choices of women and men, and discrimination. Only discrimination theories predict a wage differential between female- and male-dominated jobs once differences in productivity characteristics have been taken into account. Since empirical work has repeatedly found a large wage penalty for female-dominated jobs, adherents to the voluntary choice models have argued that these studies use a misspecified model. According to this view, insufficient variables have been included in these analyses to control for productivity and supply differences between women and men. However, serious efforts were made to incorporate these types of variables into the research presented in chapter 2. Yet, this research still found sizable underpayments for "women's work." Furthermore, when other misspecifications indicated by the occupational choice model are corrected, the estimated coefficient for the sex composition of an occupation remains significant. Thus, the voluntary choice models and their adherents have not adequately explained this severe wage penalty.

Two discrimination models—the crowding and institutional models—are also reviewed. Both argue that employer discrimination contributes to occupational segregation and the wage penalty against "women's work." This chapter finds that the crowding model offers a better explanation for wage determination in the private sector, while the institutional model of discrimination more accurately describes wage determination in the public sector. I conclude that the underpayment of "women's work" reflects discrimination, but that the form of discrimination is different in the private and public sectors. In the private sector, employers' exclusionary practices have resulted in lower market wages for "women's work." The average private sector employer may not engage in exclusionary practices today, but she or he takes advantage of a discriminatory outcome, namely lower wages for "women's work" when using prevailing wages. In the public sector, employers are paying "women's work" less than "men's work" even after controlling for prevailing wages. Hence, the average public sector employer cannot explain pay differentials between male- and female-dominated jobs by appealing to market forces.

These research findings have several legal and policy implications. First, I find that the prevailing wages of "women's work" reflect discrimination. Those employers who pay prevailing wages take advantage of discrimination against women, which means they also discriminate against women. But the consensus among the appellate courts is that Title 7 was not meant to prevent employers from using market forces to determine wages. This kind of sex discrimination will not be addressed by existing law if these appellate court decisions are upheld. New legislation will be needed to challenge this kind of discrimination. Second, if the Supreme Court upholds the general consensus among the appellate courts regarding sex-based wage discrimination lawsuits, these lawsuits will have very little, if any, effect on women's salaries in the private sector. On the other hand, I find that in the public sector "women's work" is paid significantly less than "men's work" even after controlling for productivity-related differences and market forces. Hence, sex-based wage discrimination lawsuits in the public sector could improve women's salaries. Finally, these empirical results suggest a method that plaintiffs could use in sex-based wage discrimination lawsuits to counteract a defendant's claim of paying prevailing wages.

Implementation of Comparable
Worth Policies

THE IMPLEMENTATION OF comparable worth policies consists of three basic stages: (1) conducting a job evaluation plan, (2) assessing wages, and (3) making the necessary comparable worth pay adjustments. The first two steps are generally referred to as the comparable worth study. In essence, it identifies the problem that comparable worth policies are expected to eliminate, that is, that female-dominated jobs tend to be paid less than other jobs considered comparable in terms of job requirements. Job requirements are assessed by the job evaluation plan, which determines the relative worth of jobs to a firm. The comparable worth study uses this information to determine the extent to which jobs are underpaid relative to their worth. The third step—making the necessary comparable worth pay adjustments—occurs during the implementation of comparable worth, which typically results in salary increases for jobs that are paid less than other jobs deemed comparable by the job evaluation plan.

This general outline of a comparable worth policy, however, allows for considerable variation in the actual procedures followed. Indeed, dissimilarity has occurred in each of the three basic areas of a comparable worth policy: the type of job evaluation has varied; the wage comparisons have varied; and the allocation of pay adjustments has varied.

This chapter reviews the three basic steps of a comparable worth policy and highlights the variation and arbitrary elements of these policies. It shows that some approaches to comparable worth have undermined its success. It offers guidelines for implementing a successful comparable worth policy. It identifies the political and economic conditions that have been associated with states' implementation of comparable worth. It discusses the primary actors behind the adoption of comparable worth. It concludes with a discussion of the types of comparble worth policies adopted and the estimated costs of these policies.

JOB EVALUATIONS

Job evaluations are a formal procedure for determining an internal ranking of jobs according to their relative worth to a firm. In fact, job evaluations have been defined as a "generic term covering methods of determining the relative worth of jobs."[1] Relative worth is measured by examining the requirements of a job. Thus, all job evaluation systems focus on job requirements, not the credentials or productivity of the incumbent within the job. One reason for this approach is that employers have learned to rely on structured personnel functions to regulate hiring, job performance, salaries, promotion, and dismissal. Job evaluation procedures enhance this formalization of the personnel function.

Job evaluations have been used for more than 100 years. Most sources date the first instance of job evaluations back to the U.S. Civil Service Commission in 1871.[2] After the turn of the century, a real interest began to develop with the advent of scientific management. But it was not until after World War II that job evaluations became widespread. Today, it is estimated that most large firms use job evaluations.[3] Among public sector employers, it has been found that the federal government and most state governments use these techniques as well.[4]

The Job Evaluation Methodology

A variety of job evaluation systems exist, but almost all have a similar methodology, which consists of three steps: describing the requirements of each job, assessing the relative worth of jobs to the firm, and using this information as a factor in wage determination. The first step involves collecting information about each job. This information is then used to describe a job's duties and responsibilities, as well as the working conditions under which the work is performed. The collection effort may include one or more of the following approaches: direct observation, oral interviews, or questionnaires. Direct observation or oral interviews are generally completed by trained job analysts. Questionnaires are typically filled out by the incumbent and reviewed by her or his supervisor. The personnel office generally coordinates this data collection effort with assistance from a job evaluation consultant.

The second step of a job evaluation plan determines the relative worth of jobs to the firm, and produces an internal ranking of the jobs. This is typically accomplished by the personnel office in conjunction with a job evaluation consultant. The personnel office may also use an evaluation team, consisting of employees (from the personnel office and other departments) to carry out this step. How the relative worth of jobs is determined varies depending on the job evaluation system used.

The results from the job evaluation are then used by management as an instrument in wage determination. One of management's traditional reasons for undertaking a job evaluation is to determine salaries for jobs inadequately informed by the external labor market. Employers often have job titles that are unique or quite different from other establishments. Hence, either no or insufficient market information is available. For these firms, a systematic internal job evaluation can be used to assist in determining wages for these occupations. Salaries for jobs sufficiently informed by the labor market are generally determined by the market.

Types of Job Evaluation Systems

There are four basic job evaluation systems: ranking, classification, factor comparison, and factor point methods. The first two are often referred to as "qualitative" and the latter two as "quantitative" methods. There are also unconventional methods such as "decision banding," which are variants of these traditional methods.[5] Since the decision-banding system has been used by comparable worth studies, it will also be described here.

Ranking is the simplest of the four systems. All jobs within a firm are ranked from top to bottom with respect to their "worth," although worth is rarely defined. Allocating jobs into pay grades based on an overall judgment of their comparative worth would be an example of ranking. This method of job evaluation is rarely used and has not been used in comparable worth studies.

Classification systems establish a predetermined hierarchical structure, with categories in the hierarchy delineated on the basis of such factors as the degree of skill and responsibility thought to be required on a job. Each job is ranked according to this system by comparing its attributes with the descriptions of the categories in the hierarchy. The best known classification system is the General

Schedule (GS) used by the federal government. This hierarchical structure establishes a series of pay grades, which uses a number of factors to delineate its categories. Jobs are fit into this structure after comparing their requirements to these factors.

The decision-banding method is a variant of a classification system. Hence, it too is a qualitative system in that jobs are fit into an ordinal system of predetermined grades. It differs from other classification systems in that it relies on a single factor—decision making—to delineate its broad categories, or bands. Each band is further divided into grades. These further divisions are based on additional factors besides decision making, such as the working conditions of a job, and the need for accountability. Thus, all jobs are compared to one another on the basis of only one factor, decision making. Other factors are used to rank jobs within "decision bands."

The *factor comparison* method is infrequently used because it is both cumbersome to execute and difficult to understand. It involves the following steps. First, factors used in the evaluation (called compensable factors) are selected. These factors may include knowledge and skills, accountability, and working conditions. Second, jobs are selected that have standardized duties and are commonly found in a variety of industries. These jobs, which are called "benchmark" occupations, are given a total point score that reflects their total worth. The total point score is then divided into separate scores for each compensable factor. These scores reflect a factor's contribution to the total worth of each benchmark job. Based on the benchmark jobs, a numerical scale emerges for each factor. Factor scores for the remaining jobs are then determined by locating the spot on each factor scale where it best fits. Finally, all of the factor scores are summed to create a total point score for each job.

The *factor point* method is the most widely used job evaluation plan. These plans determine the relative worth of jobs by selecting a set of factors and weights that are expected to reflect the requirements of a job. The factors generally fall into four broad categories: skill, effort, responsibility, and working conditions. Weights are applied to each factor and indicate their relative importance. Each job is rated on each factor and assigned the level of points that reflects the extent to which this factor is required on the job. Factor scores are summed for each job to produce a total point score.

There are two ways to determine the weights of a factor point plan: the a priori method and the policy-capturing method. Weights are

TABLE 4.1

Evaluations from the Minnesota Job Evaluation Study

Job Title	Know-How	Problem Solving	Account-ability	Working Conditions	Total Points	Maximum Monthly Salary (10/81)
Delivery Truck Driver	Basic vocational knowledge. No mgmt or human relation skills. (76)	Repetitive and routine thinking environment. (10)	Work closely supervised. Work has minimal impact. (16)	Occasional abnormal environmental conditions. Moderate hazards. (10)	112	$1382
Clerk Typist II	Basic vocational knowledge. No mgmt or human relation skills. (87)	Repetitive and routine thinking environment. (14)	Work closely supervised. Work has minimal impact. (16)	Office environment. Minimal physical effort and hazards. (0)	117	$1115

Sources: Minnesota Commission on the Economic Status of Women, "Pay Equity and Public Employment," 1982; Minnesota Department of Employee Relations, "Hay Point Ratings for State of Minnesota Jobs," 1984.

selected before the evaluation begins in a priori systems, such as the one used by Hay Associates, a consulting firm hired by many states that have undertaken comparable worth studies. These weights are generally not explicitly identified. Instead, a numerical scale is devised for each factor that increases as the amount of the factor required on the job expands. This numerical scale implicitly reflects the relative weight of each factor. For example, the Hay system uses "know-how" and working conditions as factors in its analysis. Know-how consists of 27 levels, ranging from 50 to 1,800 points. In contrast, the working conditions factor ranges from zero to 152 points. Hence, the minimum score allowed for know-how in the Hay system is fifty times as large as that allowed for working conditions, and the maximum score is more than ten times as large.

Table 4.1 illustrates how jobs were evaluated for the state government of Minnesota using the Hay system. These jobs were evaluated on four factors: know-how, problem-solving, accountability, and working conditions. The Delivery Truck Driver, for example, was judged to have the lowest level of skill requirements and given a score of 76 points for this factor. This job was also assigned a score of 10 for working conditions due to the job requirements of moderate lifting and infrequent exposure to poor working conditions. On the other hand, the Clerk Typist was given a slightly higher skill rating of 87, indicating some knowledge was necessary to perform this job. But the working conditions were rated as zero, implying no unpleasant working conditions. The total points for these two jobs are indicated under the total point score. These two jobs were given approximately equivalent overall ratings.

The policy-capturing system evaluates jobs on each factor, but these factors do not include implicit weights. Both the states of New York and Wisconsin used this method in their comparable worth policy. In this system all factor scores increase at equal intervals as the complexity of the factor increases. The weights for each factor are determined empirically in a multiple regression analysis, where occupational salaries are estimated as a function of their factor scores. The following equation typifies this approach:

$$s_j = \hat{a}_0 + \hat{a}_1 p_1 + \hat{a}_2 p_2 + \ldots + \hat{a}_n p_n$$

where j equals the set of occupations; s equals the occupational salary; p_i are the factor scores for each occupation; $\hat{a}_i$ are the estimated coefficients. In this case, the estimated coefficients, $\hat{a}_1, \ldots, \hat{a}_n$, are the factor weights. The weights indicate how much each factor contributes to the determination of pay. In this sense, it "captures policy."

The 1981 National Academy of Sciences (NAS) report that examined the applicability of comparable worth noted an important caveat to the policy-capturing approach.[6] It argued that policy-capturing systems, when estimating the weights with regression analysis, should control for the sex composition of the occupation. Otherwise, the estimated weights would reflect the bias in pay that may exist against female-dominated jobs.[7] They recommended two approaches to overcome this problem. First, they suggested that an employer include only male-dominated jobs when determining the factors and weights. By excluding the female-dominated jobs from the regression analysis, the employer eliminates the potential negative correlation between the gender composition of a job and the factor scores. The other approach suggested by the NAS report was to control for the gender composition of the occupation when determining the factors and weights. In other words, they suggested estimating the following salary equation:

$$s_j = \hat{c}_0 + \hat{c}_1 p_1 + \hat{c}_2 p_2 + \ldots + \hat{c}_n p_n + \hat{e}\,\%F_j.$$

These estimated coefficients reflect the contribution of each factor in determining wages after the sex composition of the job is controlled for.

A Critique of Job Evaluation Plans

Many researchers have pointed out that job evaluation procedures are problematic for the purpose of determining whether "women's work" is undervalued. Comparable worth advocates have expressed concern regarding all three steps in the job evaluation process.[8] The National Academy of Sciences reviewed these procedures for their suitability in assessing the undervaluation of female-dominated jobs and also found problems with each step.[9] Others have also noted that job evaluation procedures are inherently subjective and arbitrary.[10]

Job Evaluations Are Subjective. The first concern regarding job evaluations is that the criteria used to evaluate jobs are subjective. Because of this subjectivity, bias may occur and influence the outcome of the study. For example, the information collected about job characteristics is rarely based on objective facts, such as educational degrees, certification, or years of experience. Instead, it is based on subjective judgments about aspects of a job that are difficult to quantify. The set of factors generally used to value jobs—skills, effort, responsibility, and working conditions—are similarly amorphous and lack objective criteria. The criteria tend to be vague and broadly defined, leading to imprecise measures of a job's ranking on a particular factor.

Some analysts have expressed concern that the characteristics of the individuals involved in describing the job may influence its description.[11] For example, the data collected about a job may differ depending on the position of the individual providing the information. A job evaluation can consult three sources of information: incumbents, supervisors, or trained job analysts. Generally speaking, a job evaluation relies on only one of these sources, but using only one source may bias a job description.

Others are concerned that the rating of jobs may be affected by the attributes of the evaluator.[12] For example, the gender of the rater may influence her or his evaluation. Another factor that may affect a person's evaluation is her or his familiarity with the occupation. Union members may also evaluate jobs differently than nonunion members. Although some research has concluded that individual characteristics do not have an appreciable effect on the evaluation of jobs,[13] these conclusions are not universally accepted.[14]

Evaluation Results May Not Be Reliable.   Another issue that arises when conducting a job evaluation is the reliability of the results. Specifically, evaluators may rate jobs differently. Efforts have been made to estimate the extent to which evaluators agree on their ratings of jobs, typically referred to as inter-rater reliability. This research has shown that unreliability is a serious problem in the evaluation of specific factors.[15] Total scores are also unreliably measured by single evaluators, although total evaluations from pooled assessments of five or more independently derived judgments tend to be reliable.

Different Job Evaluations May Yield Different Results.   Several studies have investigated whether different job evaluation plans produce different job rankings. The results of these studies vary widely, with correlation coefficients between plans ranging from a low of .59 to a high of .99.[16] Madigan and Hills point out that even two job evaluation plans that have a correlation coefficient of .9 or higher still produce different job rankings.[17] They argue that the relevant question is not how great the similarity is between job evaluation plans but how large the departure from perfect agreement.

Compensable Factors and their Indicators Are Arbitrary.   Most job evaluation plans choose a set of factors upon which to determine the relative worth of jobs. Yet this decision is arbitrary. Although a standardized set of factors that includes skill, effort, responsibility, and working conditions has emerged, these factors are not universally applied. Some job evaluation systems use only one factor, while others use up to 13.

In addition, the indicators used to define the set of factors in a job evaluation have a strong influence on the outcome of a study. For example, although physical effort is usually included in a job evaluation plan, it is measured by strength requirements, not fatigue levels. Furthermore, periodic heavy-weight-lifting is typically considered harder than frequent lifting of lighter-weight objects. Another example is taken from the *Dictionary of Occupational Titles* (DOT), published by the U.S. Department of Labor. A review of this job evaluation system revealed that the following occupations were given the lowest possible skill-complexity level: Nursery School Teacher and Child Care Worker. In contrast, the job of Marine Mammal Handler was rated far superior in its skill complexity. This review concluded that such rankings occurred because the DOT did not include skills related to mothering and homemaking in its measure of skill-complexity.[18]

The Weights in a Factor Point Plan Are Arbitrary. The weights selected in an a priori factor point plan are arbitrary. This is evident in the Hay system, which includes four factors—know-how, accountability, problem solving, and working conditions—where the maximum contribution allowed for know-how is at least ten times that of working conditions. "Interpersonal skills" is included in the Hay system as a component of "know-how," but is weighted far less than other subfactors, such as "breadth of management know-how." In the past, deciding the size of relative weights was guided by an effort to predict the existing wage structure. This made sense given that the firm's purpose was to predict salaries for occupations with insufficient external labor market information. But, if the firm's purpose changes, these weights could easily change as well.

Suggestions to Limit the Arbitrary and Subjective Aspects of Job Evaluations

Existing research on job evaluation procedures suggests several methods to reduce the arbitrary and subjective nature of job evaluations, which are reviewed below. First, job evaluation plans should use closed-ended questionnaires as the primary source of information about the characteristics of jobs. This type of questionnaire frames the questions in such a way as to elicit more consistent and comparable responses, minimizing the impact of gender and linguistic differences.[19] The answers are also machine readable, eliminating the need for an evaluation team. The average scores for each job can be used to reflect the requirements of the job. These questionnaires should be completed anonymously by employees without supervisory review.

Incumbents know the requirements of their job in greater detail than their supervisor, and it may be that incumbents who do not fear reprisal are more likely to give accurate job information than those concerned about the reaction of their supervisor.[20] If open-ended questionnaires are used, then the evaluation team should have at least five evaluators who should evaluate each job independently. Furthermore, these evaluators should have different individual characteristics. In other words, a single gender or occupation group should not dominate the evaluation process.

All jobs within a firm should be evaluated by a single job evaluation plan. Rather than dividing the work force into groups of occupations and conducting different evaluations for different types of jobs, a comparable worth policy should use one job evaluation for all jobs. This would allow all jobs to be evaluated by the same criteria, making it possible to compare job requirements across different types of occupations.

The only job evaluation plan that should be used in a comparable worth policy is a factor point system. There are two reasons for this. First, to be useful in the comparable worth setting, each job must be assigned a numerical value so that relative comparisons across jobs can be made. Only quantitative methods assign point values to each job. Second, factor point plans are less subjective than other quantitative methods. Subjective judgments are reduced in these plans, in part because the indicators within each factor are defined more precisely. It should be noted that most, but not all, comparable worth policies have used a factor point method to evaluate jobs. The most notable example of a policy that did not use this method is the Minnesota school districts, which used the decision-banding method described earlier.

Factors and subfactors in the job evaluation should make visible the work required in male- and female-dominated jobs. Skills traditionally associated with "women's work" should be included as factors, and subfactors, just as skills traditionally associated with "men's work." Some argue that traditional job evaluation plans overlook skills associated with "women's work."[21] Thus, existing job evaluation plans should be reviewed to assess whether they are capturing the skills required in "women's work."

Although the selection of weights in a factor point plan is arbitrary, this arbitrariness can be reduced by using a policy-capturing method rather than an a priori system. As explained earlier, a policy-capturing approach uses the existing wage structure of an employer to determine the set of factors and weights. The job evaluation process generates factor scores for an array of compensable factors, each of which increases at equal intervals as the complexity of the factor increases. Multiple regression analysis is used to determine the weights, by estimating occupational salaries as a function of their factor scores. To reduce any potential gender bias in the employer's wage structure, an employer implementing a comparable worth policy should modify this multiple regression analysis by either including only male-dominated jobs in the analysis or adding the sex composition of the occupation as an independent factor.

SALARY ASSESSMENT

Although advocates of comparable worth have criticized job evaluation procedures for their subjective and arbitrary elements, in fact, very few comparable worth policies have changed the job description and analysis components of job evaluation plans.[22] In fact, in many cases, such as Minnesota, the job evaluation had already been conducted by management without the intention of implementing comparable worth. The difference between comparable worth studies and management's traditional use of job evaluations occurs during the evaluation of wages.

When employers use job evaluation plans as an instrument in wage determination, they first divide their work force into separate occupational groups. These occupational groups consist of jobs that have similar skill requirements or are performed in the same division of the firm. For example, a firm may divide its work force into four groups: office support, maintenance, professionals, and managers. Sometimes firms have conducted different job evaluations for each occupational group, resulting in multiple job evaluation plans for a single firm. Other times a single job evaluation plan is conducted, but wage comparisons are only made within each occupational group.

Firms have traditionally made wage comparisons within an occupational group by first adopting wages from the external labor market for benchmark occupations, which are jobs that have standardized duties and are commonly found in a variety of industries. Wages for the other jobs within this occupational group are then determined by comparing their job evaluation scores to those with external wages.

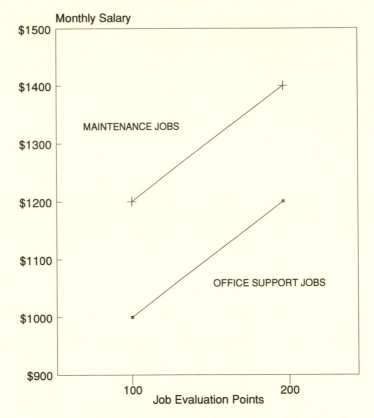

FIGURE 4.1. Separate Occupational Groups and the Resulting Pay Structure. Note: This figure illustrates management's
typical use of job evaluation results.

For example, suppose clerk/typist is selected as the benchmark occupation and its prevailing wage is $1,000 per month. All jobs within the
office support occupational group are then adjusted around that salary according to their job evaluation score in comparison to that of the
clerk/typist. On the other hand, suppose the benchmark occupation
for the maintenance occupational group is the job of delivery truck
driver and its prevailing wage is $1,200 per month. All jobs within the
maintenance occupational group are then adjusted around that salary
according to their job evaluation score in comparison to that of the
delivery truck driver. Thus, the salaries for the office support occupations and the maintenance occupations would never be compared.
Because they are in different occupational groups, the firm will pay

the truck driver $200 per month more than the clerk/typist even though the job evaluation plan rated these jobs as comparable. Figure 4.1 illustrates this situation.

Many have argued that this approach to wage determination is inappropriate when determining the undervaluation of "women's work."[23] This approach produces different relationships between job worth and pay for each occupational group. This is clearly seen in figure 4.1, where the pay line of office support jobs is well below that of maintenance jobs. Separate pay practices will exist for each occupational group if wage comparisons are not made across occupational groups. Yet, occupational groups tend to be highly sex-segregated. Thus, under this approach female-dominated jobs are typically not compared to male-dominated jobs.

Comparable Worth Approaches to Wage Determination

Employers implementing comparable worth policies have taken a very different approach to wage determination. They use the results of a job evaluation to examine a firm's salary practices for *all* jobs, regardless of their occupational group. Rather than using external wages for certain benchmark occupations, they use an internal comparison group, for example, male-dominated jobs within a firm. The salaries of female-dominated jobs are compared to the salaries of male-dominated jobs with equivalent job evaluation scores. If the female-dominated jobs are paid less than comparable male-dominated jobs, a comparable worth policy increases the salaries of the female-dominated jobs.

Four approaches have emerged among comparable worth policies to assess wages. All approaches estimate an earnings equation using ordinary least squares regression analysis. This establishes a linear relationship between pay and evaluation points that describes the firm's salary practice. The functional form and universe for this equation, however, have varied among comparable worth policies, creating the four different approaches.

The *first approach* estimates a relationship between pay and evaluation points for all jobs in a firm. This estimated regression line is referred to as the average pay line. The following equation typifies this approach:

$$s_j = a_0 + a_1 p_j + u_j \qquad (4.1)$$

where j equals the set of all jobs in a firm; s equals the occupational salary for each occupation; p is the total point score from the job evaluation for each occupation; and u is the unmeasured variation in salaries.

Figure 4.2 illustrates the average pay line. It shows the occupational salary on the vertical axis and the job evaluation score on the horizontal axis. The points on the diagram represent various occupations. The predominant sex in an occupation is determined using the 70 percent rule. The occupations are labeled as diamonds for female-dominated jobs, stars for male-dominated jobs, and boxes for balanced jobs. The average pay line is a linear representation of the relationship between pay and job evaluation points in a firm.

The disadvantage of this approach is that it does not take into account the bias in pay that may exist against female-dominated jobs. If the salaries of female-dominated jobs are less than those of other comparable jobs, then the estimated coefficients in this equation will reflect this inequity. To overcome this problem three other approaches, described below, have been used.

The *second approach* to wage determination in comparable worth policies, used by some states to overcome the weakness in the first approach, is to estimate an earnings equation for all jobs in a firm but include the sex composition of the occupation as an explanatory factor in the equation. Figure 4.3 illustrates this equation. This estimated line is called the corrected pay line. It measures the relationship between pay and evaluation points after controlling for the sex composition of the occupation. The following equation typifies this approach:

$$s_j = a_0 + a_1 p_j + a_2 \%F_j + u_j \tag{4.2}$$

where %F is the percentage of women in the occupation.

The *third approach* to wage determination, used by some states implementing comparable worth, is an estimation of the earnings equation that only includes male-dominated jobs, referred to as the male pay line. Since it is presumed that gender bias does not affect the salaries of male-dominated jobs, the linear equation predicting these salaries will not incorporate possible gender bias. Figure 4.4 illustrates this approach to wage determination in comparable worth studies. It shows an estimated line that represents a firm's salary practice for male-dominated jobs.

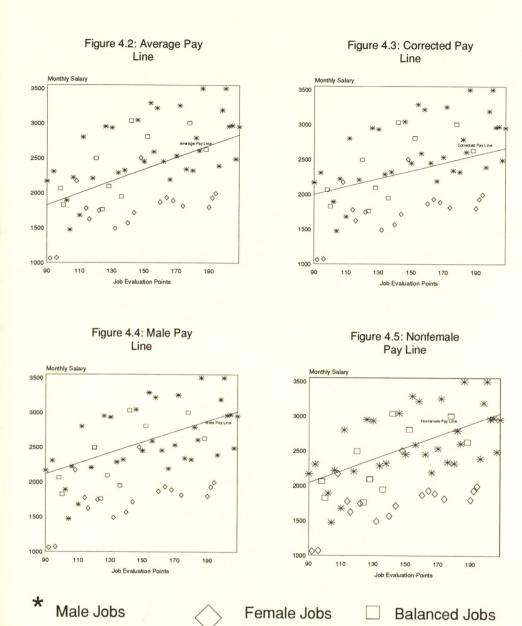

FIGURES 4.2–4.5. Four Methods for Determining Wages.

71

Figure 4.5 shows the *fourth approach* to wage determination in comparable worth studies, which estimates a pay line for non-female-dominated jobs. This approach assumes that only female-dominated jobs are potentially affected by gender bias in pay and thus only excludes these occupations from the estimation of the earnings equation. This line is called the nonfemale pay line.

Problems with Wage Determination in Comparable Worth Studies

There are at least three aspects of these wage determination procedures that are arbitrary and will affect the results of a comparable worth policy. First, the definitions used to define male- and female-dominated jobs are arbitrary. Second, the salary level used in these studies has varied, leading to different results. Third, although a functional form for the salary equation is imposed, any number of functional forms may be used, introducing yet another variation in comparable worth studies. Each of these is reviewed in greater detail below.

The Arbitrary Nature of Defining Male- and Female-Dominated Jobs. Most comparable worth policies use the so-called "70 percent rule" to define male- and female-dominated jobs, such as the states of Iowa and Wisconsin. The 70 percent rule states that female-dominated jobs are any occupation in which at least 70 percent of the employees are female, and male-dominated jobs are any occupation in which at least 70 percent of the employees are male. Although this definition has been widely used, a number of exceptions exist. For example, the state of Minnesota used the 70 percent definition for female- dominated jobs, but for male-dominated jobs it used an 80 percent rule (i.e., an occupation is male dominated if at least 80 percent of the employees are male). New York State defined female-dominated jobs as any occupation in which at least 66 percent of the employees were female.

Varying these definitions can alter the results of a comparable worth policy. If the definition of female-dominated jobs is expanded, say from a 70 to a 60 percent rule, then more jobs will be defined as female dominated. This means more jobs may benefit from the implementation of comparable worth, but the benefits to each job may be smaller. If wage determination is based exclusively on male-dominated jobs, then the pay disparity between comparable male- and female-dominated jobs will increase as the definition of a male-dominated job is narrowed, say from a 70 to an 80 percent rule, increasing the cost of implementing comparable worth.

The Arbitrary Nature of the Salary Level. Occupations are generally given a range of possible salaries, and an employee could be assigned to any one of them. Hence, the question becomes: Which occupational salary should be used in a comparable worth study? Does it make more sense to use the maximum salary, the minimum salary, or some salary step in between these two extremes?

The results of a comparable worth study may depend on which step is selected. Many people have argued that predominantly female jobs have fewer salary steps than other occupations and that their salary increments are smaller than those available to other jobs. In other words, the salaries of female-dominated jobs tend to reach their maximum step more quickly than other occupations. Nursing is the classic example of this phenomenon. Many people have argued that the nursing shortage is due in part to the fact that the maximum salaries paid to nurses are too low to keep experienced nurses from leaving the field. Hence, the maximum salaries of female-dominated jobs may be depressed further because female-dominated jobs are given fewer financial rewards for on-the-job experience.

Most comparable worth studies have used either the minimum or the maximum salary step. But, as explained above, this selection may affect the results of a comparable worth study. If only the maximum salary step is used, then comparable worth remedies will have to adjust all salary steps according to the results of the maximum salary equation. Yet, we have just seen that the maximum salary equation may produce the largest pay disparity. Hence, increasing the other salary steps by this amount would overcorrect the underpayment of female-dominated jobs. On the other hand, using only the minimum salary step in a comparable worth study may underestimate the underpayment of female-dominated jobs.

The Arbitrary Nature of the Functional Form. The functional form imposed on the aforementioned earnings equation is a linear equation. But there is no true relationship between pay and job evaluation points, so any functional form could be imposed. A log-linear function is the standard form used by economists to estimate individual earnings equations. Still other functional forms could be used.[24] For example, Hay Associates, the consulting firm mentioned earlier, often uses a kinked line to represent an employer's salary practice. This line tends to be rather steep in the lower ranges of job evaluation scores, but flattens out at higher scores. Ehrenberg and Smith examined the effect of varying the functional form of the earnings equation and concluded that this variation produced only minor changes in the results of a comparable worth study.[25] However, they only examined a few functional forms.

Suggestions to Reduce the Arbitrary Aspects
of Wage Determination

Although the definition of a female-dominated job is arbitrary, the 70 percent rule has gained legitimacy because of its ability to isolate those jobs that traditionally have been held by women. Hence, a comparable worth policy should use this definition unless an alternative one isolates these jobs more effectively. The costs involved in changing this definition when implementing comparable worth should be investigated.

Instead of analyzing only the maximum salary when determining an employer's salary practice, a comparable worth study may want to examine each salary step by estimating separate earnings equations for each salary step. Ideally, a comparable worth remedy would change each salary step for female-dominated jobs by the amount indicated from these estimated equations.

The conventional functional form for the earnings equation in a comparable worth study is a linear equation with the total job evaluation score as the independent variable. If a comparable worth study uses a different functional form, it should be justified. One method of justifying such a change is to show that the new functional form is more effective in predicting an employer's occupational earnings structure. This can be done by comparing R^2s from the new functional form and the linear functional form discussed above. The R^2 measures the amount of variation in the dependent variable that is explained by the equation. Thus, a larger R^2 means that the functional form explains more of the variation in an employer's wage structure.

CORRECTING COMPARABLE WORTH PAY DISPARITIES

A consistent finding of comparable worth studies is that even after taking job requirements into account, female-dominated jobs are paid less than other jobs found comparable by the job evaluation plan. The question then becomes: How does a comparable worth policy eliminate this pay disparity? Four approaches are described below.

The *first approach* used by comparable worth policies is to pay *every* occupation according to its job evaluation score. This approach is often referred to as the "pay for points" approach. It is achieved by paying all jobs according to the average pay line shown in figure 4.2. Jobs paid above the average pay line receive pay cuts; jobs below the average pay line receive pay increases. Female-dominated jobs are not targeted for pay adjustments under this approach. The formula for this approach is:

$$\hat{s}_j = \hat{a}_0 + \hat{a}_1 p_j \tag{4.3}$$

where $\hat{s}_j$ is the predicted pay rate for each occupation in the firm; $\hat{a}_0$ and $\hat{a}_1$ are the estimated coefficients from the least squares regression analysis; and p_j is the job evaluation score for each job.

The *second approach* is also a "pay for points" approach, but in this case all jobs are paid according to the corrected pay line shown in figure 4.3. As explained earlier, the corrected pay line controls for the possible bias in pay against female-dominated jobs when estimating the relationship between pay and points. Nonetheless, this approach does not target female-dominated jobs for pay adjustments. Instead, it decreases the salaries of all jobs above the corrected pay line and increases the salaries of all jobs below this line. The formula for determining pay under this approach is:

$$\hat{s}_j = \hat{a}_0 + \hat{a}_1 p_j + \hat{a}_2 \%\overline{F} \tag{4.4}$$

where $\%\overline{F}$ is the average sex composition of an occupation for the firm.

These two approaches are based on a definition of comparable worth that asserts that all jobs should be paid according to their worth to the firm. Most proponents of comparable worth have relied on a different definition of comparable worth, which I have adopted throughout this book, which is that female-dominated jobs should be

paid the same as male-dominated jobs of comparable value. Personnel administrators, however, have preferred the alternative definition
of comparable worth since it fits into a larger aim of theirs, to modernize classification systems and bring salaries more in line with job requirements.[26]

These pay for points approaches to comparable worth, however,
have never been enacted successfully. Workers in jobs targeted for
wage reduction, or their representatives, strongly object to these
proposals. Hence, no state has lowered the salaries of sufficiently
large numbers of jobs. Instead, a compromise is implemented,
whereby undervalued jobs receive smaller pay increases than indicated by the comparable worth study, but no occupation is subject to
a pay cut.

Most states that have implemented a comparable worth policy have
adopted this compromise approach, including Connecticut, Iowa,
Oregon, and Washington. In Iowa, for example, the consultant hired
by the state suggested the second approach, that all jobs be paid according to the corrected pay line. This meant salary cuts for hundreds
of jobs in addition to salary increases for undervalued jobs. Not surprisingly, the union representing state workers objected to this idea.
Thus, a compromise was worked out whereby undervalued jobs received smaller pay increases than originally recommended by the
consultant, but no pay cuts were administered.

The unfortunate drawback of these compromises is that they fail to
solve the problem that comparable worth policies are expected to
address. Once the salaries of undervalued jobs are increased and no
corresponding pay cuts are made for jobs above the pay line, the average and corrected pay lines shift up. If they are reestimated after the
pay adjustments are made, new pay inequities emerge. Figures 4.6
and 4.7 illustrate this problem. The compromise implementation
shifts the jobs in the lower part of the scattergram up, but there is no
corresponding shift down in jobs above the line. A new pay line
emerges and female-dominated jobs are still paid less than comparable jobs in the firm.

Another problem with these two approaches is that they extend
salary increases to all undervalued jobs rather than target female-
dominated jobs. To extend pay adjustments to all jobs goes beyond
the intent of comparable worth policies. Furthermore, it increases
the cost of implementing comparable worth since more than female-
dominated jobs receive pay increases. Some states have used the first

approach, but limited pay increases to female-dominated jobs (e.g., New York). Although this approach reduces the cost of implementing comparable worth, it does not eliminate the undervaluation of "women's work." The new average (or corrected) pay line still shifts up once salaries of predominantly female jobs are increased. Hence, female-dominated jobs may be paid according to the old average (or corrected) pay line, but their salaries will still fall short of the new average (or corrected) pay line.

Finally, these approaches rely exclusively on the job evaluation system to determine salaries, a system that is known to be inherently subjective and arbitrary. The job evaluation score is not a precise indicator of occupational pay. After all, a variety of idiosyncratic factors might legitimately affect pay. Additional variation in wages, beyond what is predicted by the job evaluation score, is expected. As long as this additional variation is not correlated with the sex composition of the job, a comparable worth policy need not eliminate it. Hence, comparable worth policies need only eliminate that variation in wages which is correlated with the sex composition of a job after accounting for differences in job requirements.

The state of Minnesota took a *third approach* to remedying pay inequities. This state implemented comparable worth by paying female-dominated jobs according to the linear equation that best described the relationship between pay and job evaluation points for male-dominated jobs. In other words, it increased the salaries of female-dominated jobs to the male pay line. Figure 4.8 illustrates this approach. The state presumed that the salaries of male-dominated jobs were unaffected by any gender bias, and thus their relationship to job evaluation points, represented by the male pay line, could be used to determine a gender-neutral method of paying female-dominated jobs. Thus, the salaries of female-dominated jobs were increased to the male pay line by the following formula:

$$\hat{s}_j = \hat{a}_0 + \hat{a}_1 p_j \qquad (4.5)$$

where $\hat{a}_0$ and $\hat{a}_1$ are estimated from a salary equation that only includes male-dominated jobs in the analysis.

Using this approach, the basic aim of comparable worth policies—to eliminate the underpayment of "women's work"—is achieved. Since female-dominated jobs are not included in the estimated earnings equation for male-dominated jobs, the male pay line does not change after the salary adjustments to female-dominated jobs. Fe-

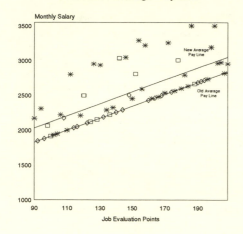

Figure 4.6: Pay Adjustments
Based on Average Pay Line

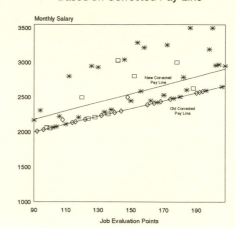

Figure 4.7: Pay Adjustments
Based on Corrected Pay Line

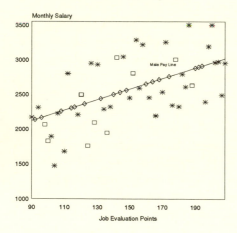

Figure 4.8: Pay Adjustments
Based on Male Pay Line

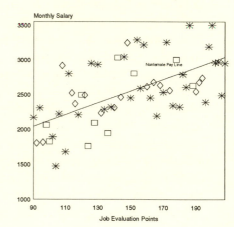

Figure 4.9: Pay Adjustments
Based on Nonfemale Pay Line

* Male Jobs ◇ Female Jobs ☐ Balanced Jobs

FIGURES 4.6–4.9. Four Methods for Adjusting Pay.

78

male-dominated jobs now receive the same pay as the average male-dominated job with the same job evaluation score. Hence, the pay inequities faced by female-dominated jobs have been completely eliminated using this approach.

Nonetheless, this approach eliminates more of the variation in wages for female-dominated jobs than is really necessary to accomplish equal pay for comparable worth. To achieve equal pay for comparable worth, pay adjustments do not have to be job specific, as they have been in the first three approaches described thus far. Job-specific pay adjustments not only eliminate the negative effect of being employed in a predominantly female job, they also eliminate the effect of any other factor other than the job evaluation score that may influence occupational salaries. For example, suppose the jobs of child care counselor and consumer specialist are both female-dominated and are considered comparable by the job evaluation system. Suppose consumer specialists are paid $8.34 an hour, while child care counselors are paid $7.20 an hour. Furthermore, suppose the average wage for comparable male-dominated jobs is $9.53 an hour.[27] The state of Minnesota would have increased the salary of consumer specialists by $1.19 and child care counselors by $2.33. But this approach eliminates *all* of the wage variation *among* comparable female-dominated jobs and relies exclusively on the job evaluation system to determine the salaries of female-dominated jobs. But, the variation in pay among comparable female-dominated jobs is not the result of gender bias and may reflect other legitimate differences that were not captured by the job evaluation system. Thus, this approach is overly reliant on the job evaluation system when determining the salaries of female-dominated jobs.

The *fourth approach*, used by the state of Wisconsin, avoids all of the weaknesses of the first three approaches. This method estimates a salary equation where all jobs are included in the analysis, but the sex composition of the job is controlled for by including a dummy variable in the equation that equals one if the job is held primarily by women and zero otherwise. This approach is similar to estimating an earnings equation for nonfemale-dominated jobs. The only advantage of estimating this equation is that the wage penalty associated with female-dominated jobs is clearly identified by the regression analysis. The following equation typifies this approach:

$$s_j = a_0 + a_1 p_j + a_2 F_j + u_j \tag{4.6}$$

where F is a dummy variable that equals one if the job is predominantly female and zero otherwise.

The comparable worth remedy for this approach is to increase the salaries of all female-dominated jobs by the absolute value of the estimated coefficient $\hat{a}_2$. This approach is illustrated in figure 4.9. The salaries of female-dominated jobs are increased, but the unmeasured component of the wage variation, u_j, is not eliminated. Thus, the salaries of female-dominated jobs as well as other jobs are still scattered about the nonfemale pay line after the implementation of comparable worth. In the example given above, both consumer specialists and child care counselors would be given the same increase in pay. In Wisconsin, each of these jobs received an increase of $1.32 an hour. Thus, their new salaries were $8.52 for child care counselors (below the average for non-female-dominated jobs) and $9.66 for consumer specialists (above the average for non-female-dominated jobs). In this way, comparable worth adjustments did not disturb the variation in pay *among* comparable female-dominated jobs. It only eliminated that pay disparity *between* comparable female-dominated jobs and other jobs.

This final approach is the most appropriate method of implementing comparable worth. It achieves the aim of comparable worth policies—paying female-dominated jobs the same as comparable male-dominated jobs—without reducing the salaries of large numbers of jobs or relying needlessly on job evaluation systems.

Guidelines for a Successful Comparable Worth Policy

Research suggests that the following guidelines for implementing a comparable worth policy will increase its success:

1. A firm should conduct a single job evaluation for all occupations within the firm. The job evaluation should be a factor point plan.

2. The factor point plan should include a wide array of job requirements, including such basic requirements as skill, effort, responsibility, and working conditions. Efforts should be made to ensure that factors relevant to "women's work" are included in the plan. Job requirements should be narrowly defined. Objective criteria should be used to evaluate job requirements. For example, instead of rating the knowledge required for a job with a scale from 1 to 10, where the categories are nebulously defined (e.g., 1 is for those who follow basic work

routines and 10 is for those who have shown unique mastery of a scientific discipline), skill should be measured by years (and months) of formal education as well as months of on-the-job training required to perform the job.

3. Job content should be based on data collected anonymously from a large number of employees from closed-ended questionnaires. If open-ended questionnaires are used, jobs should be evaluated by at least five evaluators with different individual characteristics. All of them should *not* represent the personnel office. Each evaluator should rate the jobs independently and the average score should be used as the job's point score. Evaluators should not be given information about existing salaries for jobs.

4. Weights should be determined using a policy-capturing approach that uses multiple regression analysis to estimate occupational salaries as a function of their factor scores and the sex composition of the job. For example, the following equation could be estimated:

$$s_j = a_0 + a_1 P_j + a_2 F_j$$

where j is the set of all occupations in a firm; s is the occupational salary; a_0, a_1, and a_2 are the estimated coefficients from the regression analysis; P is a vector of factor scores; F is equal to one if the job is female-dominated and zero otherwise. Female-dominated is defined as any occupation in which at least 70 percent of the incumbents are women.

5. A comparable worth policy should eliminate the likely negative effect on earnings that is associated with employment in predominantly female jobs. In other words, it should pay female-dominated jobs the same as male-dominated jobs that are deemed comparable by the job evaluation plan. This can be implemented by increasing the salaries of female-dominated jobs by the absolute value of the estimated coefficient $\hat{a}_2$.

STATES' EFFORTS TO IMPLEMENT COMPARABLE WORTH

Comparable worth initiatives for state and local public employees progressed steadily during the 1980s, despite considerable opposition at the federal level from the Reagan/Bush administrations. By 1989, 44 states had engaged in research or data collection on comparable worth, 23 states had undertaken formal comparable worth studies, and 20 states had provided comparable worth pay adjustments to at least some of their state employees.[28]

Two reasons have been given for the leadership role of state governments in the campaign for comparable worth.[29] First, state governments were more active than the federal government in adopting innovative social policies during the 1980s. Comparable worth is one example of the states' effort to fill the void regarding innovative social policies created by the federal government's inaction. Second, state legislators are more accessible to local interest groups that pushed for comparable worth. While the federal government was actively hostile toward the concept of comparable worth, feminists and union activists had access to governors and state legislators across the country with differing views on the subject, many of whom were receptive to the concept of comparable worth.

Characteristics of States that Have Enacted Comparable Worth

States that allocated funds for comparable worth tended to have three political factors in common: ratification of the federal Equal Rights Amendment (ERA), public sector unionization, and democratic control of the state.[30] For example, all but two of the twenty states that made comparable worth payments ratified the ERA.[31] Collective bargaining statutes existed in all but one of the states.[32] The Democratic party was the dominant party in all but three of the states.[33] In fact, all twenty states that made comparable worth payments met two of the three political conditions; fifteen met all three conditions.

The ERA was ratified by thirty-five states by 1982, the deadline set by Congress for its ratification. Over the next decade, all but two of these states undertook some initiative on comparable worth. But ratification of the ERA is only one measure of a state's support for women's rights. Two other measures are also correlated with the enactment of comparable worth adjustments—the proportion of women in the state House of Representatives, and whether the state has a commission on the status of women.[34] Godbey found that states with a greater proportion of women in the House of Representatives were significantly more likely to adopt comparable worth actions for state employees.[35] Evans and Nelson found that comparable worth pay raises were more likely to occur in states that had active state commissions on the status of women.[36]

Public sector bargaining is a relatively new phenomenon that gained legitimacy in 1962 when President Kennedy granted federal employees the right to unionize and bargain over working conditions, but not wages.[37] Since then most states have adopted statutes granting even broader rights to state employees; states generally permit their work force the right to unionize and bargain collectively over wages and working conditions. By 1987, only ten states remained without some form of collective bargaining for public sector employees.[38] As collective-bargaining statutes were adopted, the number of state government employees that belonged to unions increased. In 1983, 29 percent of state employees belonged to unions.[39]

This change in policy toward unionization in the public sector opened the door to greater union involvement in wage determination. The unions involved in organizing most state employees—the American Federation of State, County, and Municipal Employees and the Service Employees International Union—were actively pursuing comparable worth. This issue was viewed as a means of increasing women's pay in state government as well as attracting new members. Women represent an increasingly large proportion of the state work force. Thus, addressing women's economic issues was vital for these unions.

Comparable worth was more successful in states where Democrats exercised substantial control of the governorship, the State House (or Assembly), and the State Senate between 1981 and 1987. Although many individual Republican politicians support comparable worth, the issue is associated with the Democratic party. This was most apparent in the 1984 presidential platforms when the Democrats endorsed the concept and the Republicans denounced it. Democrats were the dominant party in forty-two states between 1981 and 1987, and all but two of these states (both southern states) took some initiative regarding comparable worth.[40]

One additional political factor has been mentioned as a precondition for the successful adoption of comparable worth—the desire to modernize and invigorate state government human resource management.[41] One might expect personnel administrators to oppose comparable worth because this policy increases payroll costs and may undermine their control of classification decisions. Instead, personnel administrators were noticeably absent from the debate over comparable worth.[42] Johansen argued that state personnel administrators did not publicly object to comparable worth because state personnel systems were politically vulnerable and needed modernization.

A series of changes took place during the 1970s that left public

personnel systems somewhat weakened.[43] First, in many states, pa-
tronage gave way to bureaucratic, merit-based personnel functions,
driven in part by increasingly complex governmental responsibilities
as well as by political considerations. The federal government threw
its weight behind this development, by enacting the Intergovernmen-
tal Personnel Act of 1970 that provided grants to states (and other
local governments) to improve their personnel systems. In addition,
most states extended collective bargaining rights to state employees
during the 1970s, further altering the personnel function. Congress
also amended Title 7 of the Civil Rights Act, which outlaws discrimination on the basis of race, color, religion, sex, or national origin.
These amendments extended Title 7 protection to state government
employees. Thus, these three major events—civil service reform, collective bargaining, and equal employment opportunity—weakened
personnel systems. This left personnel administrators vulnerable to
further alterations of personnel functions, including the additional
task of adopting equal pay for comparable worth.

States that made comparable worth pay raises also shared several
economic characteristics. Johansen found a positive correlation between states adopting comparable worth and the following two variables: (per capita) personal income and government debt.[44] She argued that wealthier states are more likely to undertake comparable
worth because they have the means to experiment with new social
policies such as comparable worth. In addition, she suggested that the
positive correlation between a state's debt and comparable worth may
reflect a state's willingness to undertake deficit spending for such
matters as increased pay for its employees.[45] Evans and Nelson found
that the states enacting comparable worth were more likely to have
progressive (in a technical sense) taxation policies and somewhat
higher state and local tax burdens.[46]

Many of the political and economic characteristics associated with
the enactment of comparable worth may actually reflect a more general tendency of some states to adopt innovative policies.[47] Walker
argued that certain states have a general tendency to adopt new policies early and that this general tendency persists over time.[48] He
found that higher levels of wealth, education, urbanization, and man-
ufacturing were consistently associated with a state's willingness to
be innovative.[49] Johansen found that an index of innovativeness
among state governments was strongly correlated with comparable
worth policy adoption.[50]

Primary Actors Supporting Comparable Worth

These political and economic characteristics may provide the necessary conditions under which a comparable worth policy is likely to occur, but successful adoption also needs actors with access to resources that can translate readiness into action.[51] These actors were drawn primarily from three areas: the women's movement, local (trade) unions, and the Democratic party, all three of which were generally necessary to achieve final adoption.

Many states had an institutionalized women's organization, like a public commission on the status of women, that provided the leadership regarding this issue (e.g., California, Connecticut, Minnesota, New York). These organizations provided critical information demonstrating the need for comparable worth for state employees. For example, the Connecticut Permanent Commission on the Status of Women investigated clerical work within the state government and found widespread sex segregation and wage inequities.[52] This led to the passage of legislation that called for a pilot study to assess the classified positions in state service. This study resulted in further legislation and ultimately about $40 million was appropriated for a complete overhaul of the state's classification and compensation system.[53]

Trade unionists, many of whom were feminists, were vocal advocates of comparable worth. Their union affiliation brought additional institutional support for the policy demand. In Oregon, for example, Margaret Hallock, Research Director of the Oregon Public Employees Union (SEIU Local 503), was a prime mover in the mobilization for comparable worth.[54] She was chair of the original Comparable Worth Task Force at her union's expense. Once the recommendations of the original task force failed to win the governor's support, she led the fight for compromise legislation that eventually resulted in $23 million for comparable worth adjustments in 1987. Without her steadfast commitment to the issue, it is doubtful that comparable worth would have been enacted in Oregon.

In certain states, feminist legislators were a principal force behind comparable worth. In Massachusetts, for example, the Caucus of Women Legislators became the institutional force for comparable worth, led by Representative Gray, after the state's commission on the status of women was abolished. In other states, sympathetic governors were instrumental in the passage of comparable worth. In Wisconsin, for example, Governor Earl, who was elected to office in 1982, was strongly committed to comparable worth. His leadership ensured the enactment of comparable worth in this state.[55]

As mentioned earlier, an important "silent" actor in the demand for comparable worth was the public personnel administrator. Rather than opposing comparable worth for increasing labor costs, in many instances public administrators viewed comparable worth as a way of gaining a new classification and compensation system.[56] In Connecticut the legislature enacted comparable worth-type legislation in 1981, in response to two preliminary studies that documented pay inequities between female- and male-dominated jobs in the state service. Yet, the legislation did not explicitly call for comparable worth, nor did it mention gender-related pay inequities as a reason for enacting the bill. Instead, it called for the Department of Administrative Services to conduct an "objective job evaluation."

This combination of demands—an objective classification and compensation system that eliminates gender inequities—was a winning combination in many states. It gave the illusion of a technical solution to a social problem. Although this combination of demands gained acceptance for comparable worth in many states, it limited its success in the implementation phase.[57] These demands encouraged states to adopt a "pay for points" approach to comparable worth. But this approach has never been fully implemented because of opposition to the proposed pay cuts. In the end, modified pay for points policies are enacted, which do not eliminate the underpayment of "women's work." For example, the Oregon legislature enacted their version of comparable worth by calling for "a single, bias-free, sex-neutral point factor job evaluation system [that] shall be applied to all jobs in state service."[58] The Comparable Worth Task Force (CWTF) concluded from this language that the salaries of *all* jobs should be adjusted to conform to the new classification system.[59] According to this view, limiting adjustments to female-dominated jobs would be considered unfair. The CWTF also wanted to use the male pay line to set the salaries for all jobs, but this was too expensive. The CWTF proposal passed the House and Senate, but was vetoed by the governor. The final comparable worth proposal, which was accepted by labor after a nine-day strike, gave wage increases to about half of the *most* undervalued jobs, defined as those 15 percent or more below the male pay line. These increases brought most undervalued jobs close to the salary range located on the average pay line, but the proposal did not include any formal goal of raising wages further than that.[60]

TABLE 4.2

Types of Comparable Worth Policies Implemented by State Governments

Type of Pay Line	Sex Type of Job Targeted by the Comparable Worth Policy		
	Female–dominated Jobs	All Jobs*	
Average Pay Line		Connecticut Hawaii Maine Oregon Ohio Vermont	Massachusetts South Dakota Washington
Corrected Pay Line	New York	Iowa	
Nonfemale Pay Line	Wisconsin		
Male Pay Line	Minnesota		

States that Have Targeted Salary Increases to Female–dominated Jobs, but Have Not Based those Increases on a Job Evaluation

California, Illinois, Michigan,
New Mexico, New Jersey, Pennsylvania, Rhode Island

Sources: National Committee on Pay Equity 1989. Chi 1986. Minnesota Commission on the Economic Status of Women 1989. Arthur Young and Co. 1987. Wisconsin Task Force on Comparable Worth 1986. Arthur Young and Co. 1984. Oregon Task Force on State Compensation and Classification Equity 1985. Tiegle 1987. U.S. GAO 1992. Massachusetts Special Committee on Comparable Worth 1988.

*Most of these states conducted a single job evaluation but did not compare jobs across different units. Maine's policy only affected the University of Maine.

Types of Comparable Worth Policies Adopted

The policy approaches used by state governments to implement comparable worth are summarized in table 4.2. This table shows that a total of twenty states have enacted some form of comparable worth. Most states used the above-mentioned modified pay for points approach to comparable worth that generally employed an average pay line to determine the extent to which jobs were undervalued, and targeted all undervalued jobs for pay adjustments. Only three states used a factor point job evaluation plan and targeted female-dominated jobs for pay adjustments. As explained earlier, two of these states, Minnesota and Wisconsin, have enacted a policy that targets female-dominated jobs and uses male-dominated (or other) jobs to determine the size of the underpayment. This is the only method that has seriously reduced the undervaluation of "women's work."

TABLE 4.3
Estimated Cost of Implementing Comparable Worth

State	Years Enacted	Total Cost	Percent of Payroll
California	1984–88	$36M	.6
Connecticut	1983–93	$40M	3.9
Iowa	1985–88	$32M	8.8*
Massachusetts	1984–89	$65M	4.1
Michigan	1985–86	$26M	.9
Minnesota	1983–86	$33M	3.7*
New York	1987	$75M	2.0*
Oregon	1987	$23M	2.4
Washington	1986–92	$115M	5.7
Wisconsin	1986–87	$57M	3.3*

Sources: Acker 1989. Dresang, n.d. Massachusetts Special Committee on Comparable Worth 1988. Minnesota Commission on the Economic Status of Women 1989. National Committee on Pay Equity 1989. Orazem and Mattila 1990. U.S. Bureau of the Census. *Public Employment* (Washington, D.C.: GPO, various years). U.S. Government Accounting Office 1992.

Note: The percent of payroll figures with an asterisk are reported in one of the sources above. The others were calculated using payroll data from the U.S. Bureau of the Census cited above.

A further approach, not yet discussed, has also been used. A number of state governments have given pay adjustments to female-dominated jobs that were not based on a comparable worth study. These states have not implemented a broad-based comparable worth policy, but are listed in table 4.2 because they have allocated funds to raise the salaries of female-dominated jobs.

Estimated Costs of Enacting Comparable Worth

Table 4.3 shows the estimated cost of implementing comparable worth for those states that spent at least $20 million on comparable worth pay adjustments. The cost of implementing this policy ranged from 0.6 to 8.8 percent of a state's payroll costs. The lowest amounts, as a percent of payroll, were spent by California and Michigan, both of which distributed pay increases to female-dominated jobs that were not based on a job evaluation plan. These two states spent about 1 percent of their payroll on comparable worth adjustments.

States that based their adjustments on a job evaluation plan spent considerably more as a percent of their state's payroll, varying from 2 to 8.8 percent of payroll. Among these states, those that targeted all jobs for comparable worth pay adjustments tended to spend more on comparable worth than those that targeted female-dominated jobs. For example, Iowa targeted all jobs for comparable worth pay adjustments and spent more as a percent of payroll than any other state, spending almost 9 percent of payroll.[61] Washington, which also distributed comparable worth pay adjustments to jobs irrespective of the predominant sex of the employees, spent the largest sum on comparable worth, $115 million, or about 6 percent of payroll. In contrast, New York's comparable worth policy, which targeted female-dominated jobs for comparable worth adjustments, only cost 2 percent of payroll. This policy, however, did not eliminate the underpayment of "women's work" as explained earlier. Minnesota and Wisconsin, two other states that targeted female-dominated jobs, spent about 3.5 percent of payroll on comparable worth. These states' comparable worth policies appear to have significantly reduced the undervaluation of "women's work," even though their costs are less than many other states enacting comparable worth.

SUMMARY

The first step of a comparable worth policy is to conduct a job evaluation, but many observers have voiced concern over the central role of job evaluation plans in comparable worth policies. Job evaluation systems are inherently subjective and arbitrary, which can lead to biased and inconsistent outcomes. Steps can be taken, however, to reduce the arbitrary and subjective nature of job evaluations, and these were listed above.

The next two steps of a comparable worth policy—evaluating wages and allocating comparable worth pay adjustments—have been enacted in different ways. These differences have occurred, in part, because of the different definitions of comparable worth. *The first definition of comparable worth is that a firm should pay female-dominated jobs the same as male-dominated jobs that are found compara-*

ble in terms of job requirements. This definition implies that female-dominated jobs should be targeted for pay adjustments and that their salaries should be compared to that of male- (or non-female-) dominated jobs. This is the kind of approach taken by the states of Minnesota and Wisconsin. *The second definition of comparable worth is that a firm should pay all jobs according to their job requirements.* Those who adhere to this definition assert that salary increases should be given to all jobs paid below the average (or corrected) pay line and that salary cuts should be given to all jobs paid above this line. This is often referred to as the pay for points approach to comparable worth.

Most states that have implemented comparable worth have adopted a compromise based on the pay for points approach, including such states as Connecticut, Iowa, Oregon, and Washington. No state has been able to adopt a pure pay for points approach. Serious objections are always raised by workers who are supposed to receive pay cuts, or their representatives. The compromise policy generally agrees to stop all salary cuts in exchange for much smaller salary increases to jobs considered underpaid.

These compromise policies are less successful and more reliant on job evaluation plans than policies based on the first definition. These compromise policies are unable to eliminate the underpayment of female-dominated jobs. They are less effective because they do not target pay adjustments to female-dominated jobs. Instead, they give adjustments to all jobs considered underpaid. Furthermore, these compromise policies rely primarily on job evaluation plans to determine salaries, yet job evaluations are inherently subjective and arbitrary. In contrast, comparable worth policies based on the first definition have succeeded in seriously reducing the gender bias in pay. Furthermore using this definition job evaluations are only needed to determine the size of the underpayment of female-dominated jobs.

Although most proponents of comparable worth adhere to the first definition of comparable worth, most states have implemented a compromise based on the pay for points approach. This has occurred, in part, because personnel administrators have tended to prefer the pay for points approach. This approach has a message that personnel administrators understand—salaries should reflect job requirements. It also fits into a larger aim that most personnel administrators have had, which is to update their classification system and bring their pay scales into line with work performed. Thus, these compromise policies typically result in a comparable worth policy that satisfies no one, but gives a little to each principal actor—unions, feminists, Democrats, and personnel administrators. In contrast, comparable worth policies like the one enacted by the state of Minnesota achieve their basic goal—to eliminate the underpayment of "women's work."

The modified pay for points approach to comparable worth also appears to be the most costly to implement, with one state spending 8.8 percent of payroll on this policy. In contrast, states that have targeted female-dominated jobs without using a job evaluation plan have spent the least amount, as a percent of payroll, on comparable worth. This approach, however, does not seriously reduce the underpayment of "women's work." States that targeted female-dominated jobs and used male- (or non-female-) dominated jobs for comparison purposes in their job evaluation plan spent about 3.5 percent of payroll on comparable worth.

The Economic Effects of
Comparable Worth

COMPARABLE WORTH POLICIES have been implemented by a number of state and local governments in the United States. Yet, the impact of this policy on the wage and employment opportunities in the jurisdictions implementing comparable worth has not been fully analyzed. This chapter reviews the anticipated effects of comparable worth policies and the empirical estimates of these effects. It then presents new estimates of the wage and employment effects of comparable worth in the state of Minnesota.

Minnesota was the first state to enact a comparable worth policy for state government employees and thus has the longest time span to reflect changes stemming from this policy. Furthermore, it is the only state that has passed legislation requiring all local governments to implement comparable worth. Comparable worth legislation for state workers was adopted in 1982, calling for salary adjustments to be given to underpaid female-dominated jobs in the state sector. These adjustments were made from July 1983 to July 1986, with salaries increasing incrementally over 4 years.

THE ANTICIPATED EFFECTS OF COMPARABLE WORTH

Below I discuss in turn, wage, employment, and other anticipated effects.

Anticipated Wage Effects

The primary effect of comparable worth will be on the pay structure of the employer enacting the policy. The basic aim of comparable worth is to increase the salaries of female-dominated jobs to the level received by other jobs deemed comparable within a firm. Hence, the first question is: To what extent has implementation achieved this goal?

The salaries of jobs not targeted by comparable worth should also be examined. Since most public sector employers give across-the-board pay increases, the salaries of nontargeted jobs will probably increase even if comparable worth is implemented. The question is: Will comparable worth affect the size of this pay increase? An employer may try to increase these salaries less than she or he would in the absence of comparable worth to pay for the higher salaries in female-dominated jobs. On the other hand, workers in these jobs and their union representatives will most likely fight against lower than anticipated salary increases. In fact, it may be that nontargeted jobs receive higher salary increases than they would have without comparable worth because an employer is compelled to keep workers in nontargeted jobs satisfied. Hence, it is not known, a priori, whether an employer will increase the salaries of nontargeted jobs more or less than would have occurred in the absence of comparable worth.

Another salary change worth examining is whether relative pay between women and men has improved. Certainly, a broader goal of comparable worth policies is to reduce the earnings disparity between women and men. Thus, examining progress toward this goal will also measure the effectiveness of comparable worth policies. Since women hold most of the jobs that are expected to receive increases under comparable worth, it is anticipated that the current pay of women will increase more than it would have otherwise. On the other hand, nontargeted jobs are expected to receive smaller pay increases than those received by targeted jobs. Since men hold most of these positions, it is anticipated that women's earnings relative to men will improve under comparable worth.

Anticipated Employment Effects

A secondary effect of increasing the wages of female-dominated jobs is that an employer may reduce employment in those jobs. Neoclassical economic theory predicts that in a competitive labor market, an employer's demand for labor will decline if the price of that labor (the wage rate) increases. Since the purpose of comparable worth is to increase the wages of female-dominated jobs, this theory predicts that once an employer adopts comparable worth, his (or her) demand for workers will fall in jobs targeted by comparable worth.

These predictions, however, may not hold under certain circumstances. For example, an employer may not necessarily respond to higher wages by minimizing costs, especially if that employer operates in the public sector and views comparable worth as a legitimate one-time increase in pay. Economists generally assume that government employers minimize labor costs because these funds have alternative uses, such as lowering taxes or financing other expenditures. But it may be that a government employer does not attempt to minimize the cost of implementing comparable worth. This outcome is more likely to occur in the following circumstances: the employer views comparable worth as a legitimate increase in labor costs; the employer's labor force is highly unionized; or the employer is currently experiencing a budget surplus and expects future revenue growth to remain strong. If management views comparable worth as a legitimate increase in labor costs, it may be more willing to finance the policy through increased revenues. On the other hand, if the labor force is highly unionized, union representatives may insist that the cost of implementing comparable worth come out of increased revenues. These views—that comparable worth is a legitimate increase in labor costs that should be financed out of increased revenues—may seem more feasible if an employer has a budget surplus at the time comparable worth is implemented.

Other Anticipated Effects

Thus far, I have only discussed the impact of comparable worth on the jurisdiction implementing this policy, but its enactment could have effects on other actors, most notably taxpayers and private sector employers. These two effects are expected to be smaller than the aforementioned impacts, but should be considered nonetheless.

A comparable worth policy may increase a jurisdiction's wage bill if it increases the salaries of female-dominated jobs without offsetting declines in employment. This increased payroll may be financed by reducing a jurisdiction's budget surplus, increasing a jurisdiction's borrowing, or increasing taxes. In the end, however, the costs are borne by the taxpayer. Hence, implementing comparable worth may increase the tax burden on taxpayers. The extent to which taxes are increased because of comparable worth can be assessed through empirical analysis.

Finally, a comparable worth policy may have indirect effects on the private sector in the community in which comparable worth is implemented. If a state government is a relatively large employer in a labor market, implementing comparable worth could affect the wage and employment opportunities in the private sector. Neoclassical economic theory suggests that implementing comparable worth in the public sector will *reduce* earnings growth in the private sector.[1] This is because comparable worth implementation should lead to fewer employment opportunities in the public sector for those female-dominated jobs that received increases. Those individuals unable to secure employment in the public sector will look for work in the private sector, increasing supply of labor to the private sector. This, in turn, will increase employment in the private sector and reduce private sector wages. Hence, public sector workers may gain from implementation of comparable worth, but private sector workers will suffer reduced earnings.

A more institutional view of the labor market, on the other hand, suggests that comparable worth implementation in the public sector will *increase* earnings in the private sector. According to this view, pay equity implementation will not substantially erode employment opportunities in the public sector. It is understood that labor demand is rather insensitive to wage increases, especially in a unionized, public sector setting. Hence, labor supply to the private sector is not increased, as neoclassical theory suggests. On the contrary, labor supply to the private sector may actually deteriorate, since individuals will be attracted to the higher salaries offered by the public sector. This attraction may cause private sector employers to match these wage increases in order to retain their workers. Consequently, wage growth may be higher in the private sector for those areas where pay equity has been implemented. In conclusion, economic theory cannot predict, a priori, whether wage growth in the private sector will be hindered or improved because of comparable worth implementation in the public sector. The only method for determining the direction and magnitude of this effect on the private sector is to examine the issue empirically.

PREVIOUS EMPIRICAL ESTIMATES

Only a few studies have attempted to measure the wage and employment effects of comparable worth. These studies can be divided into two approaches: ex ante and ex post. Ex ante studies measure the hypothetical impact of enacting comparable worth. These studies were particularly useful during the early 1980s, before comparable worth policies had been widely implemented, since they provided estimates of the likely effect of comparable worth before undertaking this policy. But now that a number of jurisdictions have enacted comparable worth policies, estimates of their impact can be measured using data that reflect their actual implementation. These studies, called ex post studies, can offer a more accurate estimate of the actual effects of comparable worth, but they must isolate its effect from other factors.

Previous Estimates of the Wage Effects

Ex Ante Studies. Ehrenberg/Smith and Sorensen conducted two ex ante studies using data from job evaluation studies from five state governments and the city of San Jose.[2] All of these jurisdictions eventually implemented some form of comparable worth policy, but the studies use salary information prior to its enactment. These studies found that if comparable worth were adopted by these jurisdictions, salaries of female-dominated jobs would increase by an average 20 percent and women's relative pay would increase by 15 percent. These authors assumed that a comparable worth policy would raise the salaries of female-dominated jobs to the level of those received by male-dominated jobs deemed comparable by a job evaluation plan. But the only state that actually implemented comparable worth in this manner was Minnesota. Most states implemented comparable worth by increasing the salaries of *all* jobs deemed undervalued by a job evaluation plan. This approach reduced the wage benefits received by women as a result of implementing comparable worth policies.

Ex Post Studies. Orazem and Mattila examined the impact of comparable worth on the pay structure of Iowa.[3] In this state, the comparable worth policy increased the salaries of *all* jobs (not just female-dominated jobs) that were paid below the corrected pay line as described in chapter 4. Because the original plan called for pay cuts as well as pay increases, the union objected to the original plan and a compromise was agreed upon that resulted in smaller gains for women in exchange for no pay cuts. This compromise severely limited the gains going directly to female workers. In fact, Orazem and Mattila argue that comparable worth increased women's pay relative to men's pay by only 1.4 percent.

O'Neill, Brien, and Cunningham examined the impact of comparable worth in the state of Washington.[4] They examined Washington State personnel files in 1983, 3 years prior to the implementation of comparable worth, and 1987, the second year of a 7-year program to phase in comparable worth salary adjustments. They found that female pay as a percentage of male pay increased 6 percentage points, from 80 to 86 percent between 1983 and 1987. They also found that the wage ratio for nonstate workers in Washington state increased 3 percentage points during the same period, half as much as that of state government workers, suggesting that comparable worth increased women's relative pay.

Killingsworth examined the wage effects of comparable worth in San Jose and Minnesota.[5] He estimated a fixed-effect model of wage determination using pooled cross-section, time-series data from the city of San Jose and the state of Minnesota. In San Jose he found that comparable worth increased the salaries of female-dominated jobs by 5.8 percentage points. In Minnesota he found that comparable worth increased women's and men's pay by 11.7 and 1.8 percentage points, respectively, increasing women's relative pay by 9.9 percentage points.

The basic problem with these analyses of the states of Washington and Minnesota is that they attempted to measure the effects of comparable worth before enactment of these policies was completed. O'Neill et al. examined data from 1987, 5 years before comparable worth was fully enacted in the state of Washington.[6] Killingsworth only included the first three of four comparable worth wage adjustments in his analysis of Minnesota.[7] Hence, these results most likely underestimate the wage effects of comparable worth in these states.

In summary, most of the work examining wage effects of comparable worth policies finds that comparable worth either increased the salaries of female-dominated jobs relative to male-dominated jobs or increased women's pay relative to men's pay. The ex ante studies predicted that comparable worth would increase women's relative pay by an average 15 percent. In contrast, the ex post studies found that comparable worth was much less successful at increasing women's relative pay.

Previous Estimates of Employment Effects

Ex Ante Studies.　Ehrenberg and Smith predicted the extent to which state and local governments would alter their employment of women if comparable worth resulted in a 20 percent increase in women's pay.[8] Using data from the 1980 Census of Population for state and local government employees, they estimated constant

97

elasticity of substitution (CES) production functions and translog cost functions to measure relevant substitution elasticities. The authors concluded that a 20 percent increase in women's pay would result in a 2 to 3 percent reduction in women's employment in these sectors.

Ex Post Studies. O'Neill et al. examined the employment effects of comparable worth in the state of Washington.[9] They found that the size of a comparable worth pay increase was negatively correlated with an occupation's share of employment growth. In other words, the higher the comparable worth wage adjustment, the lower an occupation's share of employment growth. They compared the figures from 1983–1987, a period in which comparable worth was being implemented, to figures from 1980–1983, a period prior to comparable worth, finding that this negative correlation increased after comparable worth was implemented. They concluded that the state of Washington was substituting away from occupations made more expensive by comparable worth and increasing employment in jobs not targeted by comparable worth.

Killingsworth examined the employment effects of comparable worth in San Jose and Minnesota.[10] In both cases, he estimated labor demand equations for male- and female-dominated jobs using a fixed-effects method on panel data from the jurisdictions' personnel offices. In San Jose, he found that comparable worth caused employment to decline in female-dominated jobs by 6.7 percent. In Minnesota, he concluded that comparable worth reduced employment by 4.7 percent in female-dominated jobs and 1.2 percent in male-dominated jobs.

Each of these studies, however, has serious weaknesses. In the Washington study, O'Neill et al. do not adequately control for factors other than comparable worth that may influence relative employment growth, such as the business cycle, seasonal changes, and technological factors.[11] In the San Jose and Minnesota studies, Killingsworth examines the labor demand for female- and male-dominated jobs, rather than focusing on jobs targeted by comparable worth for pay adjustments.[12]

In summary, the ex ante studies predicted minor negative employment effects from implementing comparable worth in the state and local government sector. In contrast, the ex post studies concluded that comparable worth policies have caused significant negative employment effects in the states of Minnesota and Washington as well as in the city of San Jose. These latter studies, however, suffer from design weaknesses, suggesting the need for further research in this area.

New Estimates from Minnesota

The state of Minnesota enacted comparable worth legislation for state government workers in 1982. The following year, the legislature appropriated $21.7 million for comparable worth salary adjustments. These were distributed to state government workers in July 1983 and 1984. The legislature earmarked another $11.7 million in 1985 for comparable worth salary adjustments, which were distributed in July 1985 and 1986. Hence, the state legislature allocated a total of $33.4 million to implement comparable worth, representing approximately 3.7 percent of total labor costs.[13]

The analyses presented below are based on data from the Minnesota State Department of Employee Relations. The original data includes twenty-nine quarters of individual-level data, from October 1981 to 1988.[14] Each record has information about an individual employed by the state of Minnesota, including the person's sex, age, race, tenure, hourly wage, and job classification.

Who Received Comparable Worth Adjustments

To determine how many state workers benefited from comparable worth in Minnesota, I first measured the number of people employed by the state of Minnesota in July 1983, the first quarter of comparable worth adjustments. I then added all new employees who started working for the state during subsequent quarters of adjustments. As table 5.1 shows, I found that the state of Minnesota employed a total of 42,568 individuals between July 1983 and July 1986, 35 percent of whom received a comparable worth adjustment.

Table 5.1 shows that comparable worth adjustments were given to 66 percent of the female work force and only 9 percent of the male work force. The lion's share of adjustments, 98 percent, went to workers in female-dominated jobs; only 2 percent went to workers in gender-mixed jobs.[15] The adjustments were given primarily to clerical and nonprofessional health care workers, who received 70 percent of

TABLE 5.1

The Allocation of Comparable Worth Wage Adjustments in
Minnesota State Work Force

	Number in State Work Force 1983–1986	Percent Receiving Comparable Worth Wage Adjustments	Distribution of Comparable Worth Wage Adjustments
Total Employment	42,568	35%	14,910
Gender			
Women	19,648[a]	66%	86%
Men	22,904	9%	14%
Race			
Whites	40,454	35%	96%
Minorities	1,814	35%	4%
Occupational Composition			
% Female < 30%	18,447	0%	0%
30% < % Female < 70%	8,274	4%	2%
% Female > 70%	15,847	92%	98%
Bargaining Unit			
Law Enforcement	1,853	0%	0%
Craft, Maintenance	2,800	0%	0%
Service	4,076	22%	6%
Health Care[b]	4,671	73%	23%
Clerical	7,310	96%	47%
Technical	3,349	9%	2%
Professionals	7,986	13%	7%
Supervisors	3,654	11%	3%
Other	6,232	30%	13%

Source: Minnesota state personnel data.

[a] Numbers do not add to 42,568 because of missing data.

[b] The health care bargaining unit only includes nonprofessional workers.

all comparable worth adjustments. In contrast, no one in the male-dominated occupations of craft, maintenance, or law enforcement received adjustments.

Wage Trends in Minnesota

The success of Minnesota's comparable worth policy can be measured by the extent to which it increased the female-to-male pay ratio for state workers. During the 4 years of comparable worth implementation, women's pay relative to men's pay increased dramatically

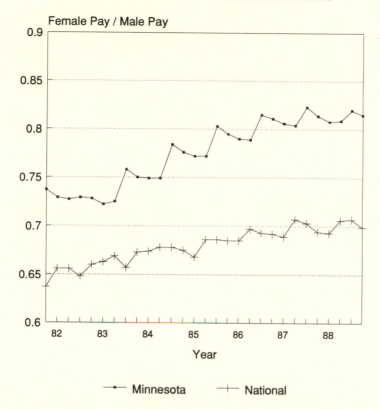

FIGURE 5.1. Women's Relative Pay: Minnesota and National Trends. Source: Elaine Sorensen, "Wage and Employment Effects of Pay Equity: Evidence from the United States." In *Policy Forum on Pay Equity: Means and Ends*, ed. Michael G. Abbott, (Kingston, Ontario: John Deutsch Institute, 1990).

for state workers. Figure 5.1 shows that prior to comparable worth in January 1983, women working for the state of Minnesota earned 72 percent as much as men. In January 1987, after 4 years of comparable worth implementation, women's relative pay increased 9 percentage points, to 81 percent. During this same period, women's pay relative to men increased nationwide by 3 percentage points, from 66 to 69 percent, about one-third of the increase for Minnesota state workers.

Although this comparison between women's relative pay in the state of Minnesota and the national trend in women's relative pay is informative, it does not control for other factors specific to the state of Minnesota that may have led to such substantial increases in women's relative pay. A statistical analysis of wage trends that controls for other factors that influence pay besides comparable worth will permit a more precise estimate of its effect on relative pay. This analysis is presented below.

Measuring Wage Effects Using Ordinary Least Squares Analyses

The first statistical analysis examined whether comparable worth reduced the wage penalty associated with being employed in a female-dominated job. In other words: Did comparable worth achieve its goal of eliminating the underpayment of "women's work"? This was achieved by estimating individual-level earnings equations 6 months before (January 1983) and 6 months after the enactment of comparable worth (January 1987). I estimated (the logarithm of) hourly pay as a function of demographic and productivity-related characteristics, including sex, race, age, current tenure, job evaluation points, and the sex composition of the job. These equations are similar to those presented in chapter 2.

These earnings equations show that the wage penalty associated with female-dominated jobs declined dramatically during the 4 years of comparable worth implementation. In January 1983, a 21 percent pay differential existed between all-male and all-female jobs after controlling for demographic and productivity differences. By January 1987, this pay differential declined to 3 percent.[16] Thus, these findings suggest that comparable worth eliminated virtually all of the pay differential between male- and female-dominated jobs.[17]

Measuring Wage Effects Using Fixed-Effects Analyses

The next analysis sought to determine how much women's pay increased relative to men's pay because of comparable worth. The statistical approach selected to answer this question was a fixed-effects method. A fixed-effects method uses panel data, which in this case consists of individuals who have repeated observations over time. This study uses personnel data from the state of Minnesota that give information about each worker on a quarterly basis from October 1981 to October 1988. In principle, an ordinary least squares regression of these data can yield consistent estimates of the parameters in the earnings equation. However, if the error term in the earnings equation tends to be the same over time for a given individual, then the estimated parameters from an ordinary least squares analysis are no longer consistent. For example, the Minnesota personnel data do not include a person's level of education, but education level is considered one of the most important predictors of a person's salary. I attempted to proxy a person's education level by including the job evaluation score for the person's job, but we do not have this information for all workers. Even if we did, a job evaluation score is a job-level variable and does not reflect each individual's abilities. Thus, a person's abilities that are not captured by the job evaluation score are included in the error term. Since these abilities probably remain the same over time for a given individual, an ordinary least squares analysis of these data will yield inconsistent parameter estimates. To the extent that this component of the error term is individual-specific and time-invariant, a fixed-effects method eliminates this component from the error term.

Fixed-effects regressions are equivalent to estimating an ordinary least squares regression with a dummy variable added for each individual in the analysis. These dummy variables control for the time-invariant individual effects, that is, they capture all time-invariant independent variables in the model, such as race and sex. Thus, these variables are dropped from the fixed-effects regression. To analyze the earnings of women and men, I estimated separate gender-specific earnings equations.[18]

Another advantage of the fixed-effects regression is that it avoids the possible effect of changes in the composition of the state's work force when estimating the effect of comparable worth. An ordinary least squares regression of these data can only control for changes in the independent variables included in the data. For example, age is included in the personnel records. Thus, an OLS regression of wages that included age as an explanatory variable would control for age. This would also control for any change in the age composition of the state work force. Thus, the effects attributable to comparable worth in this OLS regression would not be due to changes in the age composition of the work force. But an OLS regression on these data cannot control for changes in the education of the state work force because this information is missing from the personnel record. I can control for the job evaluation score of an individual's job, but this is not a perfect proxy for education, as explained earlier. It may be that the educational composition of the state work force changed in ways that

103

are not reflected in the job evaluation score. Since an OLS regression cannot control for education, the regression results may confound the effects of a changing educational distribution with the effects of comparable worth. On the other hand, a fixed-effects regression controls for time-invariant individual effects. To the extent that education is time-invariant (i.e., an employee's education does not vary while working for the state), this method controls for changes in education. Thus, the fixed-effects regression controls for any compositional change that reflects changes in time-invariant factors.

Sample Used in Analysis.   I used a representative sample of employees who had worked for the state of Minnesota during any quarter between October 1981 and October 1988. I did not restrict my sample to employees who had been employed every quarter during the entire 7-year period. Instead, any individual who had worked at least one quarter during this period could have been selected.[19] I selected a representative sample rather than use the entire file because there were almost one million personnel records in the full data set. In a fixed-effects analysis, the total number of observations is equal to the number of personnel records multiplied by the number of time periods analyzed (29 in this case), meaning the final data set would have included about 29 million observations if I had not selected a sample.

I first estimated the fixed-effects model separately for male and female workers. I then divided male and female workers into those who worked in jobs targeted for comparable worth adjustments and those not targeted for adjustments.[20] I reestimated the fixed-effects model separately for each of these groups. These latter results provided a more precise estimate of the impact of comparable worth on earnings. As explained earlier, a comparable worth policy is expected to increase the earnings of women and men in jobs targeted by comparable worth, but the extent of this increase will vary depending on the policy implemented. In addition, we do not know a priori what the impact of this policy will be on the earnings of women and men in jobs not targeted by comparable worth.

Specification of the Model.   The dependent variable is the logarithm of real hourly earnings.[21] The following explanatory factors are included in the analysis: four variables that indicate the enactment of the states' four comparable worth adjustments, current tenure, the square of current tenure, age squared, age multiplied by current tenure, the job evaluation score, the square of the job evaluation score, whether the job evaluation score is missing, a time trend, time squared, and the logarithm of real pay of private sector production workers in the state of Minnesota. The definitions of these variables are given in Appendix Table 5A.1.

The effects of comparable worth on earnings is measured by four indicator variables, CW1983—CW1986, which equal one on or after the date of the comparable worth adjustment and zero prior to that date. For example, CW1983 equals zero prior to July 1983, when the first comparable worth adjustment is made, and it equals one on July 1983 and each subsequent quarter after that date.

I control for the impact of an employee's age and tenure on earnings by including the following explanatory variables: current tenure, its square, age squared, and age multiplied by current tenure. Current tenure is defined as years of service with the Minnesota state government since the employee's most recent start date.[22] In fixed-effects models, individual characteristics that do not vary with time, such as race, drop out of the analysis. Since I included time as a control variable, any variables that increase one-for-one with time, such as age, also drop out of the analysis. But variables, such as age squared (or age multiplied by tenure), do not drop out of the analysis. In addition, current employment tenure does not necessarily increase one-for-one with time. Thus, I included it and its square as explanatory variables.

I also included a person's job evaluation score, the square of job evaluation score, and a dummy variable if the job evaluation score was missing for the person's job. These variables were added because they are strong predictors of earnings which results, in part, because these data do not include a person's education level. Earnings are expected to increase as the job evaluation score increases. The square of the job evaluation score is included because other analyses have shown that wages increase with the job evaluation score, but the size of the wage increase diminishes as the job evaluation score increases. The squared term captures this nonlinear relationship between wages and the job evaluation score. A large number of jobs do not have a job evaluation score. Rather than exclude individuals in these jobs from the analysis, I included them by adding a dummy variable to the regression that equals one if the job evaluation score is missing and zero otherwise.

The time trend terms, TIME and TIMESQ, define time in number of years, with TIME equal to zero in October 1981, the first date in the data set. TIMESQ is the square of TIME. It is included because earnings increased more rapidly during the initial period of the analysis and then increased at a slower rate during the latter period. Having both time variables in the analysis attempts to capture this nonlinear trend in earnings.

I added the logarithm of the real wage rate paid to private sector production workers in the state of Minnesota. I included this variable to control for variations in the tightness of the Minnesota labor market since wages are generally responsive to cyclical fluctuations in the local market.

Results. Table 5.2 shows that Minnesota's comparable worth policy increased women's pay by 15.0 percent relative to what would have been expected on the basis of trends and characteristics of the women.[23] On the other hand, men's pay increased by 2.8 percent during comparable worth's implementation after controlling for other factors. The impact of comparable worth on women's pay relative to men's pay was 11.9 percent.[24] All of the comparable worth indicator variables are statistically significant for women (at the 5 percent level) and all but one are statistically significant for men (the full regression results are presented in the final page of Appendix Table 5A.4).

Once women and men are divided into those receiving comparable worth adjustments and those not receiving adjustments, I find even larger gains for workers targeted for comparable worth adjustments. I found that Minnesota's comparable worth policy increased women's pay in targeted jobs by 23.6 percent and it increased men's pay in these jobs by 18.3 percent relative to what would have been expected based on trends and individual characteristics. The differences in percentage increases between women and men in targeted (and nontargeted) jobs occurred, in part, because women and men have different occupational distributions within these job categories.

I also measured the effect of comparable worth on the earnings of workers in jobs not targeted by comparable worth. From these results I can determine the effect of comparable worth on workers that are not supposed to be affected by the policy. Yet, as I explained earlier, these workers may find that their earnings increased or decreased in response to comparable worth depending on how the state responds

TABLE 5.2
Estimated Wage Effects of Comparable Worth Based on
Fixed-Effects Regressions

	Percentage Change in Wages due to Comparable Worth		
	Women	Men	Relative Gain for Women
For All Jobs	15.0%	2.8%	11.9%
In Targeted Jobs	23.6	18.3	
In Nontargeted Jobs	.5	1.2	

Sources: Minnesota state personnel data; U.S. Bureau of Labor Statistics, *Employment and Earnings*, various issues; U.S. Council of Economic Advisors, *Economic Report of the President*, various years; U.S. Bureau of Labor Statistics, mimeo.

to comparable worth. In Minnesota, women's pay in nontargeted jobs increased 0.5 percent and men's pay in these jobs increased 1.2 percent during comparable worth's implementation after controlling for other factors. None of these increases, however, were statistically significant. Thus, these results suggest that, in Minnesota, the effect of comparable worth was limited to workers in jobs targeted by comparable worth for pay adjustments.

In sum, this study shows that women working for the state of Minnesota received a large wage increase from comparable worth. Women's pay increased 15.0 percent as a result of comparable worth, while men's pay increased 2.8 percent from this policy, yielding an 11.9 percent gain in women's relative pay. These results also show that comparable worth's wage benefits were largely limited to workers in targeted jobs. Comparable worth increased women's pay in jobs targeted by comparable worth by 23.6 percent; it increased men's pay in these jobs by 18.3 percent. Women and men in nontargeted jobs, on the other hand, received a 0.5 and 1.2 percent increase in pay, respectively, as a result of comparable worth. The broader effect of comparable worth was to increase the female-to-male pay ratio eight and a half percentage points, from 72 to 80.5 percent.[25]

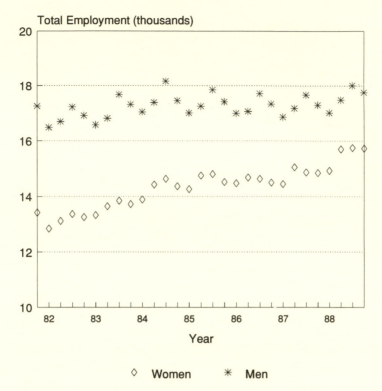

FIGURE 5.2. Employment Trends in Minnesota. Source: Same as Figure 5.1.

Comparable Worth's Effects on Employment

Women's and men's employment in the state sector of Minnesota continued to grow during the 1980s despite the additional labor costs incurred by comparable worth. Figure 5.2 shows that men's employment is quite seasonal in the state, rising in the summers and falling in the winters, but these seasonal fluctuations did not affect the overall increase in men's employment during this period. Men's employment increased from 17,251 in October 1981 to 17,757 in October 1988. There was also a clear increase in women's employment, which is less affected by seasonal change. Women's employment increased from 13,418 to 15,732 between October 1981 and October 1988. Thus, total employment in the state of Minnesota increased, from 30,669 to 33,489 between October 1981 and October 1988. These descriptive statistics suggest that comparable worth did

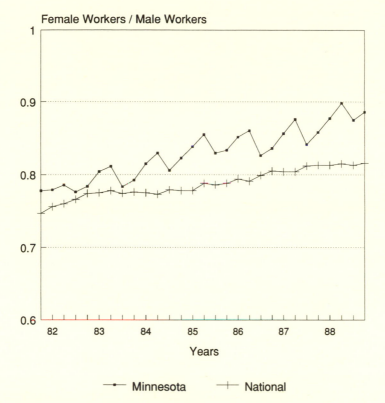

Female Workers / Male Workers

FIGURE 5.3. Relative Employment: Minnesota and National Trends. Source: Same as Figure 5.1.

not significantly reduce overall employment in the state of Minnesota. Figure 5.2 also shows that women's employment grew much faster than men's employment in the state sector of Minnesota during the 1980s.

This relative increase in women's employment is shown more clearly in figure 5.3, which presents the trend in the female-to-male employment ratio in Minnesota state service as well as in the economy as a whole. This figure shows that in October 1981, 78 women were employed by the state of Minnesota for every 100 men, yielding a .78 female/male employee ratio. By October 1988, this ratio had increased 11 percentage points to .89. In the economy as a whole, this female/male employee ratio increased from .75 to .82. Thus, the ratio increased faster for state workers in Minnesota than in the economy as a whole. These trends suggest that pay equity had no significant negative impact on women's relative employment, even though women's relative earnings increased by 12 percent.

But simple trends may be misleading. These trends do not isolate the effect of comparable worth from other factors affecting employment. To measure the impact of comparable worth on employment, a more sophisticated model is estimated, the results of which are presented below.

An Analytical Model for Measuring Employment Effects

As explained earlier, economic theory predicts that once comparable worth increases the salaries of targeted jobs, an employer's demand for workers in these jobs will decline. This relationship between wages and employment demand can be summarized by the following labor demand function:

$$\ln N_{jt} = a_0 + a_1 \ln w_{jt} + a_2 X_t + u_{jt}$$

where $\ln N_{jt}$ is the logarithm of employment in occupation j at time t, $\ln w_{jt}$ is the logarithm of hourly pay in occupation j at time t, X_t is a set of control variables, and u_{jt} is an error term. The data are longitudinal and thus the factors vary across occupations as well as over time, as reflected in the subscripts j and t.

This model of labor demand assumes that employment demand depends on the average occupational wage. In other words, it is assumed that an increase in the average wage paid to workers in a job will result in lower employment demand for that job. The coefficient a_1 measures this effect and is called the own-wage elasticity of labor demand. More precisely, it measures the percentage change in employment induced by a 1 percent change in wage. Previous research has typically found that the absolute value of this coefficient is less than one.[26]

A problem with estimating this equation using an ordinary least squares regression is that the estimated coefficient for the wage variable, a_1, will reflect the hierarchical nature of employment.[27] Employers, including state governments, tend to hire relatively few people in high-paid occupations, while employing many in low-paid occupations. Thus, we expect that employment will decline as wages rise, but this simply reflects the hierarchical nature of employment. It does not measure changes in labor demand within a job that are caused by changes in the occupational pay level.

I address the hierarchical nature of employment by estimating the labor demand function using a fixed-effects regression. If the job's position in the hierarchy is fixed, this method removes the hierarchy-induced negative relationship between jobs' pay and their employment level. In fact, this approach eliminates all occupation-specific effects that may be omitted from the analysis, including the effect of hierarchy.

Measuring Employment Effects Using a Fixed-Effects Method

The fixed-effects method in this case uses job classifications as the unit of observation with at most twenty-nine quarters of repeated observations over time. Information about job classifications were derived from personnel records from the state of Minnesota between October 1981 and October 1988. I included all job classifications in the state service during this time regardless of the length of time that the occupation existed. In other words, I did not restrict the set of jobs in the analysis in any way.

I estimated separate labor demand functions for jobs targeted by comparable worth and jobs not targeted by comparable worth. I divided jobs in this manner to isolate the employment effect of comparable worth from other factors that may influence the relationship between wages and employment in other occupations.

The dependent variable is the natural logarithm of job employment. The key explanatory variable is the mean of the natural logarithm of real wages. A time trend and its square are also included to abstract from secular trends in employment growth. To control for cyclical changes, I included the logarithm of the state's unemployment rate in the month of the personnel data as well as three months prior to that date.

I found that the wage elasticity for jobs targeted by comparable worth is −.165, but this coefficient is not statistically significant (the complete results are given in the lower right-hand panel of Appendix Table 5A.6). In other words, I did not find a statistically significant relationship between wages and employment for targeted jobs. This suggests that comparable worth had little, if any, negative effect on employment in jobs targeted by comparable worth. In contrast, the wage elasticity for jobs not targeted by comparable worth is −.620, which is statistically significant. But, as I showed above, comparable worth did not significantly affect the earnings of workers in nontargeted jobs. Thus, it appears that comparable worth had little, if any, effect on employment in jobs not targeted by comparable worth. In the end, these results suggest that employment was not significantly affected by comparable worth in the state of Minnesota.

Although these results suggest that there was no significant effect on government employment in the state of Minnesota, it would be useful to have a specific estimate of its effect. To determine a specific estimate for the impact of comparable worth on employment, I multiplied the aforementioned own-wage elasticities by the appropriate pay increases generated by comparable worth that were presented earlier. Using this method, I found that comparable worth decreased employment for women in jobs receiving comparable worth adjustments by 3.9 percent, ceteris paribus.[28] On the other hand, comparable worth decreased employment for women in jobs *not* receiving comparable worth adjustments by 0.3 percent, other things equal.[29] Hence, comparable worth caused women's overall employment to decline ceteris paribus by 2.6 percent.[30]

Using the same method described above, I found that a specific estimate of comparable worth's effect on men's employment decreased men's employment in jobs receiving comparable worth by 3.0 percent and it decreased men's employment in jobs not receiving comparable worth adjustments by 0.7 percent.[31] The overall effect of comparable worth on men's employment was to reduce it by 0.9 percent.[32]

Hence, comparable worth increased women's relative pay by 11.9 percent, which in turn led to a 1.7 percent ceteris paribus decline in women's *relative* employment. In fact, women's employment grew relative to men's employment in Minnesota state government between October 1981 and 1988. The female/male employment ratio grew from .78 to .89 during this period. But if comparable worth had not been enacted, women's relative employment would have increased another 1.7 percent to a .91 ratio.

As I mentioned earlier, government employment actually grew for women and men in the state of Minnesota during the time that comparable worth was implemented. Thus, this research does not find that individuals lost their jobs because of comparable worth. Instead, it suggests that if comparable worth had any effect on government employment, it reduced employment *growth* somewhat for women and men in the state. Based on the estimates presented earlier, I found that women's employment actually grew 17.2 percent between

October 1981 and 1988, but would have grown by 20 percent if comparable worth had not been enacted, adding about 420 jobs to the state sector. This number is small compared to the 15,000 women employed by the state of Minnesota. In addition, without comparable worth, men's employment would have grown by 3.9 percent, rather than 2.9 percent, adding about 160 jobs. Hence, comparable worth resulted in approximately 580 fewer jobs being created by the state government of Minnesota. This is a small negative effect given that the state of Minnesota employs over 30,000 people.

LIMITATIONS OF THIS ANALYSIS

There are three principal limitations of this analysis. First, I only examined the wage and employment effects of comparable worth in one jurisdiction, namely the state of Minnesota. I found that comparable worth was successfully implemented in this state, but this result does not guarantee that any other state will successfully implement comparable worth. It only shows that comparable worth *can* be successfully implemented by a state government. Other states may implement comparable worth differently than the state of Minnesota, which will alter the benefits and costs of this policy. Similarly, other states may have different economic conditions than the state of Minnesota, which may cause them to respond differently to comparable worth. A more complete understanding of the likely success of comparable worth needs further research.

Second, I only estimated labor demand functions for targeted and nontargeted jobs, ignoring possible substitution among these jobs. In other words, I assumed that once the wages of targeted jobs are increased, the employer makes no attempt to substitute other forms of labor for this relatively more expensive group of workers. There is no a priori reason to believe that an employer would avoid such substitutions. In earlier work, I estimated a translog cost function that allows for interoccupational substitution.[33] I found that comparable worth had an even smaller employment effect in Minnesota than reported here.

Third, I only examined the impact of comparable worth on the wage and employment opportunities in the jurisdiction enacting the policy. I did not analyze the effects of comparable worth on two other groups—taxpayers and private sector employers. I found that women working for the state of Minnesota gained from comparable worth without substantially decreasing government employment opportunities or negatively affecting the salaries of male government workers. But this policy increased the state's payroll, which is ultimately financed by taxes. Thus, taxes in all probability increased because of comparable worth, negatively affecting taxpayers. Furthermore, as I explained earlier, private sector salaries and employment opportunities could have been negatively affected by comparable worth. Neoclassical theory suggests that implementing comparable worth will reduce earnings growth in the private sector. In contrast, a more institutional view of the labor market predicts that comparable worth enactment in the public sector may increase earnings growth in the private sector. This is an empirical question that should be addressed by future research.

SUMMARY

This chapter first discussed the anticipated effects of comparable worth on the wages and employment opportunities within a jurisdiction implementing comparable worth policies. Previous research on the wage and employment effects of comparable worth was then reviewed and several deficiencies were found. Many of these studies analyzed the hypothetical impact of implementing comparable worth rather than its actual effect. Among those that considered actual cases of comparable worth policies, most ended their analysis before implementation was completed or used simple descriptive comparisons that could not distinguish between the effects of comparable worth and other factors. Hence, new research findings based on my analysis were presented on the wage and employment effects of comparable worth in Minnesota.

I found that Minnesota's effort to implement comparable worth was successful. It yielded substantial benefits to women and produced little, if any, negative employment effects. For Minnesota state government workers, the policy of comparable worth increased women's pay by 15 percent and men's pay by 3 percent, resulting in an 12 percent increase in women's relative pay. This increased the female/male pay ratio from 72 to 80.5 percent. At the same time, comparable worth had negligible effects on the relative employment of women, reducing women's relative employment in the state government by 1.7 percent. The overall effect of comparable worth on state government employment in Minnesota was statistically insignificant.

There are three limitations of this analysis: it only examines one state's implementation of comparable worth; it only estimates labor demand functions for targeted and nontargeted jobs, ignoring possible substitution among these jobs; and it does not examine the anticipated effects of comparable worth on taxpayers or the private sector. Future research in these areas would improve our understanding of the effects of comparable worth.

APPENDIX

Killingsworth also used a fixed-effects method to examine the effects of comparable worth in Minnesota, but his analysis suffers from several weaknesses.[34] In this appendix, I show that these weaknesses in Killingsworth's design explain, in large part, the differences in our results. This is accomplished by first reproducing his original results and then altering his model in several stages to show how each of the problems in Killingsworth's analysis contribute to our different results.

Wage Effects of Comparable Worth. Killingsworth's analysis of the wage effects of comparable worth is limited by three factors. First, he only included the first three comparable worth adjustments in his analysis.[35] Second, Killingsworth's findings are sensitive to the specification that he selected for his model. As I show below, the set of explanatory variables that Killingsworth selected for his analysis limited the effect of comparable worth. Third, Killingsworth only analyzed individuals who were employed by the state of Minnesota continuously throughout the period of his study (57 months). This is not a representative sample of the state's employees. Continuously employed individuals are older, better-paid employees who have more state service and are less likely to be employed in a predominantly female job than the average person employed by the state. Hence, Killingsworth's results do not apply to all state workers; they only apply to long-term employees.

Killingsworth estimated a fixed-effects model with the logarithm of hourly earnings as the dependent variable and the following explanatory factors: the square of employment tenure, age multiplied by em-

115

TABLE 5A.1

Definitions of Variables Used in Regression Analyses

Dependent Variables

LN(WAGE)	Logarithm of hourly pay (used in person- and job-level analyses)
LN(RWAGE)	Logarithm of real hourly pay (used in person- and job-level analyses)
LN(EMP)	Logarithm of job employment (used in job-level analysis)

Explanatory Variables in OLS and Fixed-Effects Wage Equations

FEMALE	1 if individual is female; zero otherwise
BLACK	1 if individual is black; zero otherwise
HISPANIC	1 if individual is Hispanic; zero otherwise
INDIAN	1 if individual is Native-American; zero otherwise
ASIAN	1 if individual is Asian; zero otherwise
PFEM	The proportion of women in the worker's occupation
AGE	Age of worker
AGESQ	Age of worker squared
CURTEN	Number of years in state service since most recent hire
CURTENSQ	Current tenure of worker squared
AGE and CURTEN	Age multiplied by current tenure
HANDICAPPED	Worker is handicapped
JOB POINTS	The job evaluation score for the job
POINTSSQ	The job evaluation score squared
MISSPTS	1 if job evaluation score is missing; zero otherwise

Other Explanatory Variables in Fixed-Effects Equations

CW1983-1986	1 once the comparable worth adjustments are distributed and thereafter; zero prior to the allocation
TIME	Number of years, with October 1981 equal to zero
TIMESQ	Time squared
CPI1	Current Price Index one month prior to the month of the data

TABLE 5A.1 (continued)

CPI2	Current Price Index three months prior to the month of the data
CPI3	Current Price Index six months prior to the month of the data
CPI4	Current Price Index nine months prior to the month of the data
TENURESQ	Number of years in service squared (taken from the individual's record with the earliest start date)
AGE and TEN	Age multiplied by tenure
LN(RSTPAY)	Logarithm of real hourly pay of production workers in the state of Minnesota
LN(URATE)	Logarithm of the state's unemployment rate
LN(LAG URATE)	Logarithm of the state's unemployment rate three months prior to the month of the data

ployment tenure, the consumer price index lagged one, three, six, and nine months, a time trend, time squared, and three variables that indicate the enactment of the states' first three comparable worth adjustments.[36] The definitions of these variables are given in Appendix Table 5A.1. The first two explanatory variables—tenure squared and age multiplied by tenure—are included to control for the effect of employee's age and tenure on their earnings. Employment tenure is defined as years of service with the Minnesota state government.[37]

Killingsworth included lagged price variables, time, and time squared in his analysis of wages in an attempt to abstract from cyclical and secular effects on wages. The price variables give the value of the current price index (CPI) for all urban consumers in the month immediately preceding the month of the data, as well as three, six, and nine months prior to that date.[38] The time trend terms, TIME and TIMESQ, define time in number of years, with TIME equal to zero in October 1981, the first date in the data set.[39] TIMESQ is the square of TIME. It is included because earnings increased more rapidly during the initial period of the analysis and then increased at a slower rate during the latter period.

The comparable worth wage adjustments are modeled as three indicator variables, CW1983—CW1985, which equal one on or after

TABLE 5A.2

Ordinary Least Squares Wage Regressions (absolute value of *t*-statistics in parentheses)

Variables	1983	1987
INTERCEPT	1.361	1.558
	(118.281)	(134.629)
FEMALE	−0.014	−0.009
	(5.202)	(3.785)
BLACK	0.002	0.005
	(0.219)	(0.718)
HISPANIC	0.028	0.012
	(2.485)	(1.328)
INDIAN	−0.001	0.006
	(0.096)	(0.693)
ASIAN	−0.003	0.004
	(0.254)	(0.433)
PFEM	−.209	−.033
	(54.852)	(9.715)
AGE	0.015	0.011
	(23.548)	(18.833)
AGESQ	−.1E−3	−.9E−4
	(15.442)	(11.613)
CURTEN	0.022	0.022
	(31.370)	(36.499)
CURTENSQ	−0.3E−3	−.3E−3
	(17.811)	(25.299)
AGE and CURTEN	−.2E−3	−.1E−3
	(10.617)	(8.621)
HANDICAPPED	−0.015	−0.008
	(3.708)	(2.396)
JOB POINTS	0.003	0.003
	(126.271)	(130.987)
POINTSSQ	−.1E−5	−.1E−5
	(−56.576)	(53.202)
MISSPTS	0.686	0.764
	(162.285)	(185.344)
Adjusted R^2	0.798	0.770

Source: Minnesota state personnel data.

the date of the comparable worth adjustment and zero prior to that date. For example, CW1983 equals zero prior to July 1983, when the first comparable worth adjustment is made, and it equals one on July 1983 and each subsequent quarter after that date.

Using this model specification, Killingsworth found that the first three comparable worth adjustments increased women's pay by 12.4 percent and men's pay by 1.9 percent, resulting in a 10.3 percent gain in women's relative pay.[40] These results are summarized in Appendix Table 5A.3. This table also presents the results from my replication of his model, which yields similar results.[41] I found that the first three comparable worth adjustments increased women's pay by 13.1

TABLE 5A.3

Percentage Change in Wages from Comparable Worth: Fixed-Effects
Regression Results

	Women	Men	Relative Gain for Women
Killingsworth's Results[a]	12.4%	1.9%	10.3%
Replication of his Method	13.1	2.1	10.7
Killingsworth's Model with 29 Quarters	21.4	7.0	13.5
Changes in Specification			
Change Tenure	21.5	7.0	13.6
Add Points	21.4	7.0	13.5
Change to Real Pay	15.6	.5	15.0
Add Private Pay	16.1	1.0	14.9
Change to a Representative Sample of Workers			
	15.0	2.8	11.9

Source: Minnesota state personnel data; U.S. Bureau of Labor Statistics, *Employment and Earnings*, various issues; U.S. Council of Economic Advisors, *Economic Report of the President*, various years; U.S. Bureau of Labor Statistics, mimeo.

[a] Killingsworth, *The Economics of Comparable Worth*. Killingsworth only includes whites in his fixed-effects wage analysis. He also reports his results as percentage point increases rather than percentage increases. I have adjusted his figures here to reflect percentage changes.

percent and men's pay by 2.1 percent, increasing women's pay by 10.7 percent. (My regression results are reported in Appendix Table 5A.4.)

I first extended Killingsworth's model by estimating it on data that includes all four comparable worth adjustments. I found that once all four comparable worth adjustments are included in the analysis, women's pay increased by 21.4 percent and men's pay increased by 7.0 percent as a result of comparable worth, yielding a 13.5 percent gain in women's relative pay. The fourth comparable worth adjustment increased women's relative pay by another 2.8 percentage points, which was missed in Killingsworth's original analysis.

Next, I modified Killingsworth's specification of his earnings model. Killingsworth uses two measures of an individual's human

119

TABLE 5A.4

Fixed-Effects Wage Regressions (absolute value of t-statistics in parentheses)

	Killingsworth's Model			
	Workers Continuously Employed			
	For 19 Quarters		For 29 Quarters	
	Women	Men	Women	Men
CW1983	.042	.009	.053	.011
	(16.399)	(4.731)	(33.805)	(9.387)
CW1984	.047	.005	.043	.6E-3
	(38.316)	(5.280)	(39.081)	(.671)
CW1985	.034	.007	.030	.003
	(22.043)	(6.305)	(25.843)	(3.183)
CW1986			.068	.053
			(35.047)	(35.861)
TIME	.069	.047	.022	.019
	(7.979)	(7.675)	(7.758)	(8.953)
TIMESQ	−.006	−.005	−.003	−.005
	(11.916)	(15.128)	(21.701)	(37.587)
CPI1	.005	.006	.006	.007
	(7.951)	(14.725)	(12.803)	(20.346)
CPI2	.003	.006	.008	.008
	(3.242)	(8.817)	(14.163)	(18.787)
CPI3	−.003	−.004	−.002	−.003
	(4.157)	(7.844)	(4.791)	(7.108)
CPI4	.004	.008	.003	.006
	(8.008)	(22.525)	(7.114)	(16.147)
TENURESQ	−.5E-3	−.1E-3	−.6E-3	−.2E-3
	(25.853)	(9.514)	(42.883)	(19.456)
AGE and TEN	−.2E-3	−.4E-3	.3E-4	−.1E-3
	(10.019)	(28.371)	(3.562)	(13.067)

capital—tenure squared and age multiplied by tenure. I replaced these two measures with four different measures of human capital— current tenure, current tenure squared, age squared, and age multiplied by current tenure. Killingsworth used a measure of employment tenure that is based on the earliest date of entry to state service recorded for each person. This is an imprecise measure of a person's employment with the state, because the data do not indicate the very first start date with the government, nor do they include start and end dates for each term of employment service. Since Killingsworth's measure of employment tenure is an imprecise measure of total state service, I prefer to use current employment tenure with the state, which is accurately measured. Current employment tenure does not necessarily increase one-for-one with time as Killingsworth's measure

TABLE 5A.4 (continued)

Specification Changes to Restricted Data from 29 Quarters

	Change Measure of Tenure and Age		Add Job Evaluation Score	
	Women	Men	Women	Men
CW1983	.054	.011	.053	.011
	(33.862)	(9.249)	(35.339)	(9.803)
CW1984	.043	.0004	.043	.5E-3
	(38.980)	(.486)	(41.410)	(.652)
CW1985	.030	.003	.030	.003
	(25.865)	(2.955)	(27.219)	(3.383)
CW1986	.068	.053	.068	.053
	(34.742)	(35.473)	(36.743)	(37.125)
TIME	.029	.013	.026	.011
	(9.132)	(5.639)	(8.611)	(4.883)
TIMESQ	-.003	-.004	-.003	-.004
	(20.691)	(35.449)	(21.927)	(37.360)
CPI1	.006	.007	.006	.007
	(12.640)	(19.713)	(13.352)	(20.606)
CPI2	.008	.009	.008	.009
	(14.105)	(18.945)	(14.960)	(19.800)
CPI3	-.002	-.003	-.002	-.002
	(4.769)	(6.808)	(5.076)	(16.795)
CPI4	.003	.006	.003	.005
	(6.964)	(15.988)	(6.683)	(16.320)
CURTEN	.003	.021	.001	.020
	(1.963)	(33.355)	(1.119)	(33.051)
CURTENSQ	-.7E-3	-.1E-3	-.6E-3	-.1E-3
	(32.931)	(13.109)	(31.748)	(13.000)
AGESQ	-.2E-3	-.4E-4	-.2E-3	-.2E-4
	(12.255)	(4.206)	(11.523)	(2.478)
AGE and CURTEN	.2E-3	-.3E-3	.2E-3	-.3E-3
	(6.697)	(18.693)	(7.482)	(18.843)
JOB POINTS			.001	.8E-3
			(51.188)	(48.755)
POINTSSQ			-.1E-5	-.5E-6
			(35.176)	(28.806)
MISSPTS			.271	.209
			(57.715)	(57.320)

of employment tenure. Thus, I included it and its square as explanatory variables. I also included age squared, which is essentially equal to Killingsworth's tenure squared variable. Killingsworth's tenure variable increases one-for-one with time, just as age squared does. Thus, only one of the squared variables can be included in the analysis, either age squared or tenure squared.

This modification of Killingsworth's model—changing the selection of tenure—does not change the results that measure comparable worth's effect on earnings. Using these alternative measures of

TABLE 5A.4 (continued)

	Specification Changes to Restricted Data from 29 Quarters			
	Change to Real Pay		Add Private Pay	
	Women	Men	Women	Men
CW1983	.035	−.010	.037	−.006
	(28.264)	(10.398)	(26.440)	(5.609)
CW1984	.047	.002	.050	.006
	(48.299)	(2.051)	(40.897)	(5.841)
CW1985	.016	−.013	.015	−.015
	(17.301)	(17.820)	(14.904)	(19.151)
CW1986	.047	.026	.047	.025
	(45.466)	(32.359)	(44.766)	(31.377)
TIME	.052	.058	.049	.053
	(33.414	(59.933)	(28.269)	(47.016)
TIMESQ	−.003	−.005	−.003	−.004
	(31.343)	(60.960)	(16.340)	(31.912)
CURTEN	.001	.020	.001	.020
	(1.037)	(32.543)	(1.042)	(32.574)
CURTENSQ	−.6E−3	−.1E−3	−.6E−3	−.1E−3
	(31.552)	(12.972)	(31.552)	(12.951)
AGESQ	−.2E−3	−.2E−4	−.2E−3	−.2E−4
	(11.514)	(2.599)	(11.509)	(2.577)
AGE and CURTEN	.2E−3	−.3E−3	.2E−3	−.3E−3
	(7.513)	(18.502)	(7.507)	(18.535)
JOB POINTS	.001	.0008	.001	.8E−3
	(50.935)	48.464)	(50.958)	(48.490)
POINTSSQ	−.2E−5	−.5E−6	−.1E−5	−.5E−6
	(35.015)	(28.738)	(35.045)	(28.767)
MISSPTS	.272	.210	.271	.210
	(57.516)	(56.992)	(57.504)	(56.989)
LN(RSTPAY)			.106	.155
			(3.714)	(7.003)

human capital, I found that comparable worth increased women's pay by 21.5 percent and men's pay by 7.0 percent.

The second change in Killingsworth's specification was to add the following explanatory variables: the person's job evaluation score, the square of job evaluation score, and a dummy variable if the job evaluation score was missing for the person's job. These variables were added because they are strong predictors of earnings that result, in part, because these data do not include a person's education level. However, adding these variables to the analysis does not alter the effects of comparable worth on women's and men's pay. Appendix Table 5A.3 shows that the cumulative effect of comparable worth is

TABLE 5A.4 (continued)

All Specification Changes to Representative Sample from 29 Quarters

	Women	Men	Targeted Jobs Women	Targeted Jobs Men	Nontargeted Jobs Women	Nontargeted Jobs Men
CW1983	.032	.001	.058	.044	−.009	−.004
	(28.182)	(.997)	(54.574)	(11.377)	(3.466)	(3.209)
CW1984	.049	.012	.073	.061	.007	.007
	(48.982)	(12.139)	(77.448)	(17.708)	(3.272)	(6.827)
CW1985	.014	−.012	.028	.014	−.019	−.015
	(17.297)	(14.334)	(36.917)	(5.034)	(10.850)	(18.314)
CW1986	.045	.027	.053	.049	.026	.024
	(55.425)	(31.697)	(68.637)	(17.374)	(14.823)	(27.078)
TIME	.030	.046	.014	.032	.068	.050
	(26.988)	(39.292)	(13.805)	(7.407)	(26.386)	(41.658)
TIMESQ	−.002	−.003	−.001	−.002	−.003	−.003
	(13.551)	(20.098)	(12.628)	(3.758)	(10.991)	(22.592)
CURTEN	.017	−.8E−4	.020	.011	.016	−.8E−4
	(29.876)	(10.523)	(36.935)	(3.188)	(12.166)	(10.212)
CURTENSQ	−.6E−3	.020	−.5E−3	−.3E−3	−.5E−3	.019
	(47.363)	(28.444)	(48.367)	(5.892)	(19.459)	(25.636)
AGESQ	−.8E−4	−.3E−3	−.4E−4	−.8E−4	−.2E−3	−.3E−3
	(13.539)	(23.220)	(7.845)	(1.928)	(11.216)	(19.038)
AGE and CURTEN	.3E−4	−.2E−3	−.2E−4	−.1E−3	−.7E−4	−.2E−3
	(2.286)	(9.954)	(1.438)	(1.125)	(2.203)	(9.568)
POINTS	.001	.6E−3	.003	.004	.8E−3	.6E−3
	(67.960)	(44.080)	(64.222)	(13.681)	(18.245)	(36.097)
POINTSSQ	−.1E−5	−.4E−6	−.3E−5	−.8E−5	−.5E−6	−.3E−06
	(48.082)	(25.304)	(31.700)	(8.657)	(11.055)	(19.262)
MISSPTS	.203	.089	.385	.471	.130	.084
	(60.546)	(28.791)	(70.211)	(16.663)	(16.271)	(24.737)
LN(RSTPAY)	.164	.223	.093	.167	.296	.203
	(7.220)	(9.678)	(4.364)	(2.149)	(6.081)	(8.459)

Sources: Minnesota state personnel data; U.S. Bureau of Labor Statistics, *Employment and Earnings*, various issues; U.S. Council of Economic Advisors, *Economic Report of the President*, various years; U.S. Bureau of Labor Statistics, mimeo.

exactly the same with this specification as with Killingsworth's original specification.

The next specification change was to analyze the logarithm of real hourly pay rather than nominal pay and to delete the four price variables as explanatory variables. The method of controlling for price changes is not theoretically based. It seemed simpler to analyze real pay rather than to control for several different levels of the current price index (CPI), especially since the selection of which months of the CPI to use as controls was arbitrary.

This change in the specification of price controls substantially altered the effects of comparable worth on women's and men's earnings. Using this specification, I found that comparable worth increased women's pay by 15.6 percent and men's pay by 0.5 percent. Thus, this specification suggests that comparable worth had essentially no effect on men's pay and it increased women's relative pay by 15 percent.

The final change in specification was to add a variable that measures the change in real private sector wages. I added the logarithm of the real wage rate paid to production workers in the state of Minnesota. Adding this variable did not alter the effects of comparable worth on earnings. Women's relative pay still increased by 14.9 percent.

As explained earlier, the other basic problem with Killingsworth's analysis is that he restricted his analysis to workers who were present during the entire period covered by the data. In other words, they had to be employed by the state from October 1981 to April 1986 in order to be included in Killingsworth's analysis. These workers are not typical of all state employees. Instead, they are long-term employees, having worked for the state of Minnesota for at least 4 years. Comparable worth is designed to benefit a certain kind of worker, namely those employed in undervalued female-dominated jobs. Workers in these jobs are underrepresented in Killingsworth's sample. In addition, their gains from comparable worth are not comparable to those received by long-term employees.

The effects of comparable worth on pay are significantly altered when a representative sample of Minnesota employees is used rather than a restricted sample of long-term employees. Using a representative sample, I found that comparable worth increased women's pay by 15.0 percent instead of 16.1 percent. This suggests that comparable worth may have benefited long-term female employees slightly more than short-term female employees. On the other hand, using a representative sample shows that comparable worth increased men's pay by 2.8 percent rather than the 1.0 percent that was estimated by Killingsworth's sample. This suggests that short-term male employees benefited more from comparable worth than long-term male employees. Nonetheless, the gain in women's relative pay is now estimated at 11.9 percent rather than the 14.9 percent arrived at using Killingsworth's restricted sample.

In sum, I found that all three weaknesses of Killingsworth's design—limiting his analysis to the first three comparable worth adjustments, selecting a specification that limited comparable worth's effect, and restricting his sample to employees who were employed by the state for at least 57 months—contributed to our different results regarding the effects of comparable worth on earnings in Minnesota.

Employment Effects of Comparable Worth. Killingsworth used a fixed-effects method to analyze the employment effects of comparable worth, just as I have done, but his analysis is limited by two problems. First, Killingsworth only included occupations that employed workers throughout the period of analysis, that is, his sample is restricted to occupations with positive employment in every quarter between October 1981 and April 1986. But this means his sample of occupations tends to include those occupations with a large number of employees. Occupations with relatively few workers are more likely to be vacant for a short period than occupations with a large number of workers. Since larger occupations tend to be lower paid, his sample includes a disproportionate number of larger, lower-paid jobs. Thus, he does not use a representative sample of occupations to estimate his labor demand functions. It is unclear, however, what impact this restrictive sample will have on his estimates of the wage elasticities for female- and male-dominated jobs.

Second, Killingsworth did not estimate separate labor demand functions for jobs targeted and not targeted by comparable worth. Instead, he estimated labor demand functions for jobs that are female-dominated and male-dominated (in October 1981).[42] These categories do not correspond to the set of jobs affected by comparable worth. Female-dominated jobs include a larger number of jobs, many of which were not targeted for comparable worth adjustments. Furthermore, many of the jobs targeted by comparable worth were not female-dominated in October 1981, when Killingsworth determined the gender composition of each job. In other words, his sample of female-dominated jobs included many jobs that were not targeted for comparable worth adjustments and excluded many jobs that were targeted. Thus, examining the labor demand for female-dominated jobs does not accurately measure the effect of comparable worth on state employment.

To correct these two problems, I first replicated Killingsworth's model using nineteen quarters of data for jobs that have positive employment throughout the period. I then changed the sample to include all jobs in the state service and to include twenty-nine quarters

TABLE 5A.5
Estimated Wage Elasticities from Fixed-Effects Employment Regressions

	Female–Dominated Jobs	Male–Dominated Jobs
Killingsworth's Results[a]	−.40*	−.64*
Replication of his Method	−.28*	−.57*
Killingsworth's Model on All Jobs in 29 Quarters	−.48*	−.56*

	Targeted Jobs	Nontargeted Jobs
Change to Targeted/ Nontargeted Jobs	−.12	−.63*
Change to Real Pay	−.16	−.62*
Add Unemployment Rate	−.17	−.62*

Sources: Minnesota state personnel data; U.S. Bureau of Labor Statistics, *Employment and Earnings*, various issues; U.S. Council of Economic Advisors, *Economic Report of the President*, various years; U.S. Bureau of Labor Statistics, mimeo.

* Statistically significant at the 5 percent level (two-tailed test).

[a] Killingsworth, *The Economics of Comparable Worth*.

of data from October 1981 to October 1988, a period that includes all four comparable worth adjustments. Using this more inclusive sample, I separated the sample into targeted and nontargeted jobs rather than female- and male-dominated jobs. Finally, I changed the set of explanatory variables for the model to determine whether the results are sensitive to model specification. These results are summarized in Appendix Table 5A.5. The complete regression results are presented in Appendix Table 5A.6.

In Killingsworth's labor demand function, the dependent variable is the natural logarithm of job employment. Wages are measured by the mean of the natural logarithm of wages.[43] In his basic model, the control variables are a time trend, time squared, and four measures of the consumer price index.[44] Killingsworth included the time trend variables to abstract from cyclical and secular trends in employment growth. The price controls are included because Killingsworth measured wages in nominal terms. It is generally believed that labor de-

TABLE 5A.6
Fixed-Effects Employment Regressions (absolute value of t-statistics in parentheses)

	Killingsworth's Model			
	Jobs Continuously Present for 19 Quarters		All Jobs in 29 Quarters	
	Female Job	Male Job	Female Job	Male Job
LN(WAGE)	−.283 (2.538)	−.569 (12.287)	−.484 (6.950)	−.555 (15.476)
TIME	.033 (.506)	.081 (3.054)	.027 (1.179)	.044 (4.295)
TIMESQ	−.007 (1.728)	−.005 (3.108)	−.003 (2.209)	−.001 (1.604)
CPI1	.007 (.804)	.003 (.899)	.015 (2.815)	−.001 (.486)
CPI2	−.012 (.817)	.001 9.234)	−.003 (.558)	−.001 (.429)
CPI3	.012 (1.053)	−.006 (1.363)	−.001 (.238)	.5E−3 (.159)
CPI4	.002 (.181)	−.002 (.566)	.001 (.194)	.002 (.639)

	Specification Changes to Data with All Jobs in 29 Quarters					
	Change to Targeted Jobs		Change to Real Wage		Add Unemployment Rate	
	Targeted Job	Nontargeted Job	Targeted Job	Nontargeted Job	Targeted Job	Nontargeted Job
LN(RWAGE)			−.155 (1.433)	−.622 (18.910)	−.165 (1.515)	−.620 (18.805)
LN(WAGE)	−.119 (1.071)	−.633 (19.073)				
TIME	−.032 (.928)	.035 (3.638)	.013 (1.170)	.019 (6.772)	.014 (1.218)	.022 (7.574)
TIMESQ	.3E−3 (.157)	.8E−3 (1.464)	.2E−3 (.143)	−.4E−3 (1.039)	−.4E−3 (.286)	−.001 (3.306)
CPI1	.014 (1.765)	.001 (.600)				
CPI2	−.004 (.470)	−.001 (.497)				
CPI3	−.8E−3 (.083)	.001 (.481)				
CPI4	.004 (.504)	.001 (.535)				
LN(URATE)					−.043 (1.751)	−.023 (3.193)
LN(LAG URATE)					.009 (.367)	−.024 (3.468)

Sources: Minnesota state personnel data; U.S. Bureau of Labor Statistics, *Employment and Earnings*, various issues; U.S. Council of Economic Advisors, *Economic Report of the President*, various years; U.S. Bureau of Labor Statistics, mimeo.

127

mand responds to real wages rather than to nominal values. Hence, Killingsworth added the price control variables to control for price inflation. Labor demand is expected to increase if wages are held constant and the consumer price index rises because the real cost of labor will be lower.

Killingsworth found a significantly negative relation between pay and the level of employment with jobs for female- and male-dominated jobs. His results implied wage elasticities of about −.4 and −.63 for predominantly female and male jobs, respectively. According to Killingsworth, employment growth in predominantly female and male jobs would have been 4.7 and 1.2 percent higher if comparable worth had not been implemented. Employment continued to grow despite the enactment of comparable worth. Thus, no one lost their job as a result of comparable worth. But Killingsworth estimated that subsequent employment growth was significantly smaller than would otherwise have been the case.

I duplicated Killingsworth's sample and used his model specification, but I was unable to replicate Killingsworth's results for the estimated labor demand functions for female- and male-dominated jobs. My estimated wage elasticities were slightly smaller in absolute terms than those estimated by Killingsworth. The wage elasticities were −.28 and −.57 for female- and male-dominated jobs, respectively, which are reported in Appendix Table 5A.5.[45]

Once I expanded the sample to include all jobs in the twenty-nine quarters between October 1981 and October 1988, the estimated wage elasticities increased in absolute terms. The wage elasticities for female- and male-dominated jobs using this expanded sample were −.48 and −.56, respectively. In other words, I found that using a more representative sample of occupations increased the value of the estimated wage elasticities (in absolute terms) for Minnesota state employees in female- and male-dominated jobs. This suggests that Killingsworth underestimated the extent to which the Minnesota state government responded to higher wages in female- and male-dominated jobs.

Next, I estimated labor demand functions for targeted and non-targeted jobs rather than female- and male-dominated occupations. This change in the categorization of jobs resulted in a significantly different picture than that presented by Killingsworth. Once the jobs targeted by comparable worth were isolated from other jobs, I found that the wage elasticity for these jobs is −.12, which is no longer significantly negative and considerably smaller (in absolute terms) than the estimated elasticity for female-dominated jobs. In contrast, the wage elasticity for jobs *not* targeted by comparable worth is −.63, which is significantly negative and similar in value to the wage elasticity for male-dominated jobs. These findings suggest that comparable worth had little, if any, negative effect on the employment in the state of Minnesota. Thus, they show the importance of accurately identifying the occupations targeted by comparable worth for pay increases before estimating wage elasticities to assess the impact of comparable worth.

I also changed the set of explanatory variables used in the analysis to determine whether the results were sensitive to the specification of the model. First, I replaced the nominal value for mean wages with the real value and I deleted the price control variables from the equation.[46] This change simplified the specification and employed the same wage variable that I adopted for the wage equations presented earlier. I then added two additional explanatory variables that attempt to capture the state of the economy in Minnesota. These variables give the logarithm of the state's unemployment rate in the month of the personnel data as well as 3 months prior to that date. These specification changes altered the results slightly, but the basic findings remained the same. The wage elasticity for targeted jobs is now −.17, but it is still statistically insignificant; the wage elasticity for nontargeted jobs is now −.62 and still significantly negative.

In sum, I found that two limitations of Killingsworth's analysis of the employment effects of comparable worth—restricting the sample of occupations to those that had positive employment throughout the period and estimating wage elasticities for female- and male-dominated jobs rather than targeted and nontargeted jobs—contributed to our different results.

Conclusions and Policy Recommendations

A Serious Problem Exists

ALTHOUGH the gender pay gap declined in the 1980s, women working full-time still earned 70 percent less than men in 1991. A significant portion of this pay gap is the result of occupational segregation in the labor market. In 1991, over half of female workers were concentrated in three traditionally female fields—clerical, sales, and service work; only one in five worked in blue-collar jobs or managerial positions, the occupations in which most men worked. A broad range of empirical research almost universally shows that occupational segregation in the labor market results in lower pay for "women's work." This kind of pay inequity is responsible for approximately 27 percent of the total pay gap between women and men.

After reviewing the economic literature on pay differentials and conducting original research on this topic, I conclude that this underpayment of "women's work" results from economic discrimination against women. This does not imply intent on the part of employers. Economic discrimination exists when workers of one sex are denied economic opportunities available to workers of another sex for reasons that have little or nothing to do with their individual abilities.

I find that the crowding model of discrimination provides the best explanation of the discrimination process in the private sector. According to this theory, employers discriminate against women by excluding them from occupations considered "men's work," which in turn increases their supply and reduces their salaries in other occupations, typically referred to as "women's work." Hence, the lower pay in "women's work" reflects discrimination. A specific employer may not engage in these discriminatory practices, but she or he takes advantage of a discriminatory outcome by paying prevailing wages for "women's work."

In contrast, the discrimination process in the public sector is better characterized by the institutional model of discrimination. Here, the underpayment of "women's work" does not solely reflect the use of prevailing wages from the external labor market. On the contrary, even after prevailing wage are taken into account, I find that "women's work" is significantly underpaid in the public sector. This suggests that institutional factors specific to the public sector contribute to the underpayment of "women's work."

POTENTIAL WEAKNESSES OF A COMPARABLE WORTH POLICY

The purpose of comparable worth policies is to eliminate intrafirm pay discrepancies between male- and female-dominated jobs that are not accounted for by differences in job requirements. Policy implementation consists of three basic steps: conducting a job evaluation plan, assessing wages, and making the necessary comparable worth wage adjustments.

Many have voiced concern over the central role of job evaluations in comparable worth policies. They note that job evaluation plans are inherently subjective and arbitrary. But steps can be taken to reduce the negative aspects of job evaluation plans, which are outlined in chapter 4.

Two basic approaches to enacting comparable worth have emerged: the "pay for points" approach and the Minnesota-type approach. The "pay for points" approach asserts that all jobs should be paid according to their job evaluation score. Thus, jobs currently overpaid according to the job evaluation plan are targeted for pay cuts; those underpaid are expected to receive pay increases. A *pure* "pay for points" approach, however, has never been implemented because the workers who are employed in the jobs destined for pay cuts, or their representatives, strongly object to it. Instead, a compromise is implemented where smaller pay increases are given to underpaid jobs, but no pay cuts are administered.

This compromise "pay for points" approach has three serious weaknesses: (1) it does not achieve the basic purpose of comparable worth—to eliminate the underpayment of "women's work"; (2) it does not target pay adjustments to female-dominated jobs; and (3) it is overly dependent on the job evaluation system. This approach cannot achieve equal pay for comparable worth because it relies on pay cuts to achieve this aim, but these cuts are never enacted. By targeting all underpaid jobs for pay adjustments, this approach increases the cost of comparable worth and undercuts the gains to female workers. Finally, it relies primarily on the job evaluation system to determine

131

salaries, a system that is known to be subjective and arbitrary. A comparable worth policy only needs to eliminate the variation in wages that is negatively correlated with the "femaleness" of a job once job requirements are taken into account. This approach tries to eliminate *all* wage variation once job requirements are accounted for.

In contrast, the Minnesota-type approach avoids these weaknesses. It achieves the basic goal of comparable worth by targeting female-dominated jobs for wage adjustments, which eliminate the underpayment of "women's work." It only needs a job evaluation plan to assess the size of this underpayment. It does not rely on the job evaluation plan to determine the salaries of all jobs.

WAGE AND EMPLOYMENT EFFECTS OF COMPARABLE WORTH

The primary effect of comparable worth is on the pay structure of the employer enacting the policy. The basic aim of comparable worth is to eliminate the pay discrepancy between predominantly male and female jobs that have comparable job requirements. Hence, the first question is: To what extent has implementation achieved this goal? A broader goal of comparable worth policies is to reduce the earnings disparity between women and men. Thus, progress on this front also measures the effectiveness of the policy. The salaries of jobs not targeted for comparable worth should also be examined to determine whether these salaries have been altered to offset the cost of comparable worth.

Secondary consequences of this policy may include alteration of the employment opportunities in the jurisdiction enacting comparable worth. Neoclassical theory predicts that an employer will decrease employment in those jobs that receive comparable worth pay adjustments. Other secondary effects of comparable worth include its impact on taxpayers and private sector employers.

In the case of Minnesota, I find that the comparable worth policy was quite successful. It practically eliminated the entire pay disparity between male- and female-dominated jobs that is unaccounted for by differences in job requirements. The wage penalty associated with female-dominated jobs declined from 21 to 3 percent during the implementation of comparable worth. This policy was also quite successful in increasing the female-to-male pay from 72 to 80.5 percent, representing a 12 percent increase in women's relative pay. Furthermore, the state of Minnesota did not offset the cost of comparable worth by reducing the wage growth of its male work force. On the contrary, comparable worth resulted in a 3 percent increase in men's pay and a 15 percent increase in women's pay. Finally, comparable worth had negligible effects on state government employment. Women's and men's employment continued to grow during the enactment of comparable worth, but this policy reduced their employment growth by 2.6 and 0.9 percent, respectively, reducing women's relative employment by 1.7 percent.

The Minnesota case, however, represents only one successful implementation of a comparable worth policy. Many other states that implemented comparable worth do not appear to have had this kind of success. Success depends, in part, on the method of implementation and the economic conditions at the time of enactment. Furthermore, I did not examine the effect of comparable worth on taxpayers or private sector employers, who also may be negatively affected by comparable worth. Future research should examine these effects as well as the wage and employment effects of comparable worth.

The Future of Comparable Worth

Comparable worth will undoubtedly continue to be implemented by state and local governments either through legislation, administrative order, or collective bargaining. But these efforts will tend to be relatively small. The bigger question is: What will the U.S. Supreme Court and the U.S. Congress do regarding this issue?

Its Future in the Courts. Ten years ago, advocates of comparable worth had hoped to advance the concept of comparable worth through the legal system. This hope emerged because of the 1981 Supreme Court decision known as the *Gunther* decision, ruling that sex-based wage discrimination under Title 7 was not limited to equal work cases. Since then, however, several appellate courts have ruled that plaintiffs in these cases cannot use the disparate impact standard to establish discrimination. Instead, they must show intentional discrimination. Furthermore, they have ruled that market forces are a legitimate defense against an initial or prima facie showing of discrimination. Hence, plaintiffs must show that this defense is merely a pretext for discrimination.

Under these restrictions, public sector employers are still vulnerable to sex-based wage discrimination lawsuits. I present statistical evidence on the public sector that shows female-dominated jobs are paid less than male-dominated jobs even after controlling for productivity differences and market forces. Plaintiffs must still establish a prima facie case of intentional discrimination. In addition, they must show that the public sector employer's appeal to market forces is inaccurate. I suggest a statistical method for arguing this point in chapter 3.

In contrast, most plaintiffs suing private sector employers will not be able to establish discrimination under these restrictions. Research presented in chapter 3 shows that the pay disparity between male- and female-dominated jobs is eliminated in the private sector once prevailing wages are taken into account. Since the appellate courts are accepting market forces as a legitimate defense in Title 7 wage discrimination cases, plaintiffs will be unable to prove discrimination against the average private sector employer.

It is not clear how the Supreme Court will rule on future cases alleging sex-based wage discrimination under Title 7. Five new justices were added to the Supreme Court since the *Gunther* decision in 1981 by Presidents Reagan and Bush. These members, along with Chief Justice Rehnquist, provide a 6–3 majority that could uphold lower court decisions that have restricted these cases. It could even decide to overturn *Gunther* and limit sex-based wage discrimination lawsuits under Title 7 to equal work cases. Under either scenario, litigation as a means of achieving equal pay for comparable work will no longer be a viable option.

Its Legislative Future.   The Congress has been relatively supportive of comparable worth policies. Legislation to conduct a comparable worth study of the federal job classification system passed the House of Representatives several times during the 1980s, but similar bills introduced in the Senate were never formally voted on. At the request of the Congress, the General Accounting Office (GAO) has begun a study of the federal government's pay and classification systems to determine whether gender bias exists in these systems.

There are several reasons why the federal government should enact a comparable worth policy. First, original research presented in chapter 3 shows that governments pay "women's work" significantly less than "men's work" even after controlling for productivity differ-

134

ences and market forces. This strongly suggests that the federal government's current pay and classification systems treat "women's work" and "men's work" differently.

The second reason the federal government should enact a comparable worth policy is that the gains to female employees do not have to be offset by serious negative effects. The state of Minnesota has implemented this policy with negligible negative effects. Public sector employers are not forced to minimize costs to the extent that private sector firms are. Although it is true that taxpayers ultimately determine the size of government, providing a constraint to government costs, governments do not face the kind of competitive pressure from other suppliers as do private firms. Hence, governments can more easily absorb a one-time increase in payroll costs, which is how comparable worth policies are generally implemented.

Finally, a comparable worth policy is quite compatible with the federal government's existing salary administration. The federal government has a highly structured salary system made up of grades and steps that each employee must follow. This system is quite isolated from the external labor market. Salary surveys of the private sector may be conducted for a small portion of its jobs, but many government jobs have no private sector counterparts. Hence, internal equity and job requirements already play a large role in wage determination in the federal government.

In the United States a comparable worth policy in the private sector could be implemented by extending Executive Order 11246. This executive order requires that federal contractors take affirmative action in hiring and promoting members of protected classes. In late 1980, the Carter administration's Office for Federal Contract Compliance, the federal agency that enforces the executive order, proposed revisions that would have contained comparable worth language. The revisions stated: "The contractor's wage schedules must not be related to or based on the sex of the employees."[1] These proposed revisions were dropped shortly after President Reagan took office. However, the proposed regulations remain open to a future administration with a different orientation.

Extending Executive Order 11246 to require enactment of comparable worth by federal contractors would result in partial coverage of the private sector by a comparable worth mandate. Several economists have noted that partial coverage of the private sector by a comparable worth policy may have negative wage and employment effects on workers in the uncovered sector.[2] Fewer workers may be hired in the covered sector due to higher wages required by a comparable worth policy. These displaced workers could then end up in the sector of the economy not covered by comparable worth. This increase in the supply of workers could result in higher unemployment and lower wages in the uncovered sector. Such results depend, in part, on the labor demand elasticities within and between the covered and uncovered sectors, elasticities that are currently unknown. Hence, extension of comparable worth to the private sector should depend, in part, on further research into the possible negative effects of a policy's partial coverage of the private sector.

Federal legislation requiring all private sector employers to implement comparable worth is not likely in the United States. Nonetheless, our neighbor to the north, the Province of Ontario, has already implemented such a policy, which is being phased in between January 1990 and 1994. Policymakers in the United States can learn a great deal from Ontario's experience with comparable worth. Evidence of its economic effects can shed light on the likely effects of extending comparable worth to the private sector in the United States.

SUMMARY

In conclusion, a serious problem exists in the U.S. labor market in that women are paid less than men for comparable work. In the public sector, comparable worth policies have been implemented successfully—they have improved the relative economic position of women without causing significant employment loss—suggesting comparable worth is a worthy policy. But these implementations have been the exception rather than the rule. Certain procedures, outlined in chapter 4, should be followed to reduce the weaknesses of this policy. Extending it to other public jurisdictions, such as the federal government, could be beneficial if implemented appropriately. Any federally mandated extension of comparable worth to the private sector should first examine the outcomes of the Ontario Province comparable worth policy that covers both the private and public sectors. When extending comparable worth to the private sector, other issues related to the partial coverage of the private sector under a comparable worth policy should also be considered.

✣ Notes ✣

CHAPTER ONE

1. Comparable worth and pay equity policies have become interchangeable terms, both referring to policies that reduce the pay discrepancy between male- and female-dominated jobs. Sometimes, however, pay equity refers to a broader goal than equal pay for comparable worth. To avoid confusion, this book tends to use the term comparable worth rather than pay equity.

2. Treiman, Donald J., and Heidi I. Hartmann, eds., *Women, Work, and Wages: Equal Pay for Jobs of Equal Value* (Washington, D.C.: National Academy Press, 1981).

3. U.S. Bureau of Labor Statistics, *Handbook of Labor Statistics*, Bulletin 2340 (Washington, D.C.: GPO, 1989), 26; U.S. Bureau of Labor Statistics, *Employment and Earnings* (January 1992), 163.

4. Sar A. Levitan, Peter E. Carlson, and Isaac Shapiro. *Protecting American Workers* (Washington, D.C.: Bureau of National Affairs, 1986).

5. Ronnie Steinberg, "'A Want of Harmony': Perspectives on Wage Discrimination and Comparable Worth," in *Comparable Worth and Wage Discrimination*, ed. Helen Remick (Philadelphia: Temple University Press, 1984), 3–27.

6. Treiman and Hartmann, *Women, Work, and Wages*.

7. Treiman and Hartmann, *Women, Work, and Wages*, 33. This analysis has a number of problems, as other researchers have pointed out (for example, Aldrich and Buchele 1986). The most serious drawback, however, is that it does not control for the differences in productivity characteristics between women and men before measuring the impact of occupational segregation on earnings. Most empirical work on this issue finds that the male/female earnings gap is partly due to different productivity characteristics between women and men. For example, the average male worker has more work experience than the average female worker and this differential explains part of the earnings disparity between women and men. Since the NAS result does not take productivity differences into account, its findings must be viewed as an overestimate of the impact of occupational segregation on earnings.

8. Treiman and Hartmann, *Women, Work, and Wages*, 28.

9. June O'Neill, "An Argument Against Comparable Worth," in *Comparable Worth: Issue for the 80's*, vol. 1, ed. U.S. Commission on Civil Rights (Washington, D.C.: U.S. Commission on Civil Rights, 1984), 177.

10. Male occupational earnings were excluded from the analysis in order to focus on the underpayment that women experience while employed in female-dominated jobs. Farming occupations and private household occupations were deleted from this example to focus the discussion on jobs that are more likely to include a large percentage of workers who are wage and salaried workers. If all occupations are included, the lowest paid occupation for full-time working women was domestic child care worker and the average hourly pay was $3.48 in 1990.

11. This particular analysis suffers from two drawbacks that will be discussed in greater detail in the next chapter. In fact, most of the earlier work on this topic was subject to these flaws, including the work conducted by the National Academy of Sciences discussed earlier. Nonetheless, the purpose of this discussion is not to offer definitive estimates of the underpayment, but to introduce the concept so that a more sophisticated analysis that provides more precise estimates could be undertaken in the next chapter.

12. *New York Times*, 26 October 1979, A20.

13. National Committee on Pay Equity, *Pay Equity Activity in the Public Sector: 1979–1989* (Washington, D.C.: National Committee on Pay Equity, 1989).

14. U.S. General Accounting Office, *Pay Equity: Washington State's Efforts to Address Comparable Worth* (Washington, D.C.: GAO, 1992), 26.

15. *New York Times*, 17 November 1984, 15.

16. Robert E. Livernash, *Comparable Worth: Issues and Alternatives* (Washington, D.C.: Equal Employment Advisory Council, 1980); Phyllis Schafly, ed., *Equal Pay for UNequal Work* (Washington, D.C.: Eagle Forum Education and Legal Defense Fund, 1984).

17. National Committee on Pay Equity, *Pay Equity*, 1989.

18. *Daily Labor Reporter* (BNA), no. 71, 12 April 1985, E-1.

19. *Daily Labor Reporter* (BNA), no. 112, 11 June 1985, D-1.

20. U.S. Office of Personnel Management, *Comparable Worth for Federal Jobs* OPM Document 149-4-3 (Washington, D.C.: OPM, 1987).

21. National Committee on Pay Equity, *Pay Equity*, 1989.

22. National Committee on Pay Equity, *Pay Equity*, 1989.

23. Minnesota Commission on the Economic Status of Women, *Pay Equity: The Minnesota Experience* (Minnesota: Minnesota Commission on the Economic Status of Women, 1989).

24. Robert G. Gregory and Anne E. Daly, "Can Economic Theory Explain Why Australian Women Are So Well Paid Relative To Their U.S. Counterparts?" mimeo.

25. Mark Killingsworth (1990a) argues that these policies had no long-term effect on women's relative pay, but Gregory and Daly (1991) refute this finding using the same methodology as Killingsworth but with a slightly different empirical specification of the policy phases.

26. Patricia McDermott, "Pay Equity in Canada: Assessing the Commitment to Reducing the Wage Gap," in *Just Wages: A Feminist Assessment of Pay Equity*, eds. Judy Fudge and Patricia McDermott (Ontario: University of Toronto Press, 1991), 21–32.

27. National Committee on Pay Equity, *Legislating Pay Equity* (Washington, D.C.: National Committee on Pay Equity, 1990).

28. Roberta Robb, "Equal Pay for Work of Equal Value in Ontario: An Overview," in *Policy Forum on Pay Equity: Means and Ends*, ed. Michael G. Abbott (Queens University, Kingston, Ontario: John Deutsch Institute for the Study of Economic Policy, 1990), 16–20.

29. National Committee on Pay Equity, *Legislating Pay Equity*, 1990.

30. Bureau of National Affairs, *The Comparable Worth Issue* (Washington, D.C.: Bureau of National Affairs, 1981).

31. Isabelle Katz Pinzler and Deborah Ellis, "Wage Discrimination and Comparable Worth: A Legal Perspective," *Journal of Social Issues* 45:4 (1989), 51–66.

32. *Wards Cove Packing Co. v. Atonio*, 57 U.S.L.W. 4584 (1989).

33. West Publishing Co., *United States Code Congressional and Administration News* 102nd Congress—First Session vol. 1 (Minnesota: West Publishing Co., 1992): Public Law 102–166, p. 1074.

34. Paul Weiler, "The Wages of Sex: The Uses and Limits of Comparable Worth," *Harvard Law Review* 99:8 (1986), 1728–1807.

35. *American Nurses Association v. State of Illinois*, 783 F. 2d 716 (7th Cir. 1986).

36. *AFSCME v. State of Washington*, 770 F.2d 1401 (1985).

37. William Scheibal, "AFSCME v. Washington: The Continued Viability of Title VII Comparable Worth Actions," *Public Personnel Management* 17 (Fall 1988): 315–22.

38. *Corning Glass Works v. Brennan*, 417 U.S. 188 (1974).

39. Helen Remick, "Major Issues in A Priori Applications," in *Comparable Worth and Wage Discrimination*, ed. Helen Remick (Philadelphia: Temple University Press, 1984), 99–117.

40. *AFSCME v. State of Washington* (1985).

CHAPTER TWO

1. This definition is derived from the following work: Gary Becker, *The Economics of Discrimination* (Chicago: University of Chicago Press, 1957); Ronald Oaxaca, "Male-Female Wage Differentials in Urban Labor Markets," *International Economic Review* 14 (October 1973): 693–709; Francine Blau and Marianne A. Ferber, "Discrimination: Empirical Evidence from the United States," *American Economic Review* 77 (1987): 316–20.

2. Ronald Oaxaca, "Male-Female Wage Differentials."

3. See the following for a similar definition of discrimination. Blau and Ferber, "Discrimination," Glen G. Cain, "The Economic Analysis of Labor Market Discrimination: A Survey," in *Handbook of Labor Economics* vol. 1, eds. Orley Ashenfelter and Richard Layard (Netherlands: Elsevier Science, 1986), 693–785.

4. Donald J. Treiman and Heidi I. Hartmann, eds., *Women, Work, and Wages: Equal Pay for Jobs of Equal Value* (Washington, D.C.: National Academy Press, 1981).

5. David Snyder and Paula M. Hudis, "The Sex Differential in Earnings: A Further Reappraisal," *Industrial and Labor Relations Review* 32 (1979): 378–84; Treiman and Hartmann, eds. *Women, Work, and Wages,*

6. Marianne Ferber and Helen M. Lowry, "The Sex Differential in Earnings: A Reappraisal," *Industrial and Labor Relations Review* 29 (1976): 377–87; Paula England, Marilyn Chassie, and Linda McCormack, "Skill Demands and Earnings in Female and Male Occupations," *Sociology and Social Research* 66 (1982): 147–68.

7. Mark Aldrich and Robert Buchele, *The Economics of Comparable Worth* (Cambridge, Massachusetts: Ballinger, 1986); June O'Neill, "The Determinants and Wage Effects of Occupational Segregation," The Urban Institute, 1983.

8. O'Neill, "Determinants and Wage Effects."

9. Aldrich and Buchele, *The Economics of Comparable Worth.*

10. Randall Filer, "Occupational Segregation, Compensating Differentials and Comparable Worth," in *Pay Equity: Empirical Inquiries*, eds. Robert T. Michael, et al. (Washington, D.C.: National Academy Press, 1989), 153–70.

11. This example was first noted by Jim Smith; see Michael et al., *Pay Equity: Empirical Inquiries*, 174.

12. Paula England, *Comparable Worth: Theories and Evidence* (New York: Aldine De Gruyter, 1992).

13. U.S. Bureau of the Census, "Male-Female Differences in Work Experience, Occupation, and Earnings: 1984," *Current Population Reports*, Series P-70, No. 10 (Washington, D.C.: Government Printing Office, 1987).

14. Francine D. Blau and Andrea H. Beller, "Trends in Earnings Differentials by Gender: 1971–1981," *Industrial and Labor Relations Review* 41 (1988): 513–29.

15. U.S. Bureau of the Census, "Male-Female Differences in Work Experience, 1984."

16. Elaine Sorensen, "Measuring the Effect of Occupational Sex and Race Composition on Earnings," in *Pay Equity: Empirical Inquiries*, eds. Robert T. Michael, et al. (Washington, D.C.: National Academy Press, 1989), 101–24.

17. Gregory B. Lewis and Mark A. Emmert, "The Sexual Division of Labor in Federal Employment," *Social Science Quarterly* 67 (March 1986): 143–55; Peter F. Orazem and J. Peter Mattila, "Comparable Worth and the Structure of Earnings: The Iowa Case," in *Pay Equity: Empirical Inquiries*, eds. Robert T. Michael, et al. (Washington, D.C.: National Academy Press, 1989), 179–99; Mark R. Killingsworth, *The Economics of Comparable Worth* (Kalamazoo: W.E. Upjohn Institute, 1990).

18. Gregory B. Lewis and Mark A. Emmert, "The Sexual Division of Labor."

19. Orazem and Mattila, "Comparable Worth and the Structure of Earnings: The Iowa Case."

20. Killingsworth, *The Economics of Comparable Worth*.

21. George Johnson and Gary Solon, "Estimates of the Direct Effects of Comparable Worth Policy," *American Economic Review* 76 (1986): 1117–25.

22. U.S. Bureau of the Census, "Detailed Occupation and Years of School Completed by Age for the Civilian Labor Force by Sex, Race, and Spanish Origin: 1980," PC80-S1–8 (Washington, D.C.: Government Printing Office, 1983). Unlike the 1983 CPS data (which use 1980 census occupational categories), the PSID data use occupational categories from the 1970 census. Thus, the proportion of women in each occupation was calculated from 1980 census data and then converted into 1970 categories using a conversion table developed by the U.S. Census (1986).

23. Ann R. Miller, Donald J. Treiman, Pamela S. Cain, and Patricia A. Roos, eds., *Work, Jobs, and Occupations: A Critical Review of the Dictionary of Occupational Titles* (Washington, D.C.: National Academy Press, 1980).

24. The PSID only asks a respondent about the number of years a person has worked since she or he was 18 when the individual becomes the head of a family or the wife of a head (i.e., only when a new family is formed). After that time, the work experience variable must be updated, adding annual hours worked from each subsequent year through 1984. More information regarding the construction of this variable is available from the author upon request. In addition, it should be noted that in most survey years, the husband answered questions regarding his wife's labor force participation.

25. U.S. Bureau of the Census, "Male-Female Differences in Work Experience, Occupation, and Earnings: 1984;" Francine D. Blau and Andrea H. Beller, "Trends in Earnings Differentials by Gender: 1971–1981."

26. U.S. Bureau of the Census, "Male-Female Differences in Work Experience, Occupation, and Earnings: 1984"; Blau and Beller, "Trends in Earnings Differentials."

27. Aldrich and Buchele, *The Economics of Comparable Worth*, England, *Comparable Worth: Theories and Evidence*; Randall Filer, "Occupational Segregation, Compensating Differentials and Comparable Worth"; O'Neill, "Determinants and Wage Effects."

28. Johnson and Solon, "Estimates of the Direct Effects of Comparable Worth Policy."

29. Blau and Beller, "Trends in Earnings Differentials by Gender: 1971–1981."

30. For example, the correlation between the variable F and tenure is equal to −.04 for men and −.05 for women. The correlations between F and firm size are even smaller than these figures. In contrast, the correlation between F and whether an individual works part-time is equal to .18 for men and .12 for women. This suggests that a variable measuring the proportion of part-time workers in an individual's occupation is more correlated than tenure or firm size with the variable F.

31. Johnson and Solon, "Estimates of the Direct Effects of Comparable Worth Policy," 12.

32. Blau and Ferber, "Discrimination: Empirical Evidence from the United States."

33. Cain, "The Economic Analysis of Labor Market Discrimination."

CHAPTER THREE

1. Francine D. Blau and Marianne A. Ferber, "Discrimination: Empirical Evidence from the United States," *American Economic Review* 77 (1987): 316–20; Glen G. Cain, "The Economic Analysis of Labor Market Discrimination: A Survey," in *Handbook of Labor Economics* vol. 1, ed. Orley Ashenfelter and Richard Layard (Netherlands: Elsevier Science, 1986), 693–785; Ronald Oaxaca, "Male-Female Wage Differentials in Urban Labor Markets," *International Economic Review* 14 (1973): 696–709.

2. Charles Brown, "Equalizing Differences in the Labor Market," *The Quarterly Journal of Economics* (February 1980): 113–34.

3. Francine D. Blau and Andrea H. Beller, "Trends in Earnings Differentials by Gender, 1971–1981," *Industrial and Labor Relations Review* 41 (1988): 513–29; Paula England, George Farkas, Barbara Kilbourne, and Thomas Dou, "Explaining Occupational Segregation and Wages: Findings from a Model with Fixed Effects," *American Sociological Review* 53 (1988): 544–58; Elaine Sorensen, "Measuring the Pay Disparity Between Typically Female Occupations and Other Jobs: A Bivariate Selectivity Approach." *Industrial and Labor Relations Review* 42 (July 1989): 634–39.

4. Blau and Beller, "Trends in Earnings Differentials by Gender, 1971–1981."

5. England, et al., "Explaining Occupational Segregation and Wages."

6. Gerhart and Cheikh also conducted a fixed-effects analysis of earnings and the sex composition of the occupation. They found no significant effect

from the sex composition of the job on female earnings. But this study only analyzed women who were in their twenties, which is not a representative sample of working women. Barry Gerhart and Nabil El Cheikh, "Earnings and Percentage Female: A Longitudinal Study," *Industrial Relations* 30 (1991): 62–78.

7. Sorensen, "Measuring the Pay Disparity Between Typically Female Occupations and Other Jobs: A Bivariate Selectivity Approach."

8. There are other models of discrimination, most notably that developed by Becker (1957). However, Becker did not posit that occupational segregation contributed to the earnings disparity between women and men. Nonetheless, occupational segregation can be introduced into these models (see Aldrich and Buchele 1986, or Blau 1984). Yet, these modified theories predict that women experience wage discrimination if they enter predominantly male jobs, not if they enter predominantly female jobs. Thus, they do not predict an underpayment for "women's work." According to these models, the only way that wages in female-dominated jobs could be affected by discrimination is if women leave male-dominated jobs and crowd into female-dominated jobs, the same mechanism described in the crowding hypothesis. Thus, these models do not provide an additional theoretical explanation for lower wages in female-dominated jobs. Consequently, they are not reviewed here.

9. Francine D. Blau and Carol Jusenius, "Economists' Approaches to Sex Segregation in the Labor Market: An Appraisal," in *Women and the Workplace: The Implications of Occupational Segregation.* ed. Martha Blaxall and Barbara Reagan (Chicago: University of Chicago Press, 1976), 181–99; Donald J. Treiman and Heidi I. Hartmann, eds., *Women, Work, and Wages: Equal Pay for Jobs of Equal Value,* 1981; Ray Marshall and Beth Paulin, "The Employment and Earnings of Women: The Comparable Worth Debate," in *Comparable Worth: Issue for the 80's* vol. 1, ed. U.S. Commission on Civil Rights (Washington, D.C.: U.S. Commission on Civil Rights, 1984), 196–214.

10. See, for example, Robert T. Averitt, *The Dual Economy* (New York: W. W. Norton and Co., 1968); Peter B. Doeringer and Michael J. Piore, *Internal Labor Markets and Manpower Analysis* (Massachusetts: D.C. Heath and Company, 1971).

11. Barbara R. Bergmann, "Occupational Segregation, Wages and Profits When Employers Discriminate by Race and Sex," *Eastern Economic Journal* 1 (April/July 1974): 103–10.

12. Robert T. Averitt, *The Dual Economy.*

13. E. M. Beck, Patrick M. Horan, and Charles M. Tolbert II, "Stratification in a Dual Economy: A Sectoral Model of Earnings Determination," *American Sociological Review* 43 (October 1978): 704–20.

Chapter Four

1. Brian Livy, *Job Evaluation: A Critical Review* (New York: John Wiley and Sons, 1975), 13.

2. Donald J. Treiman, *Job Evaluation: An Analytic Review* (Washington, D.C.: National Academy of Sciences, 1979).

3. Dov Elizur, *Systematic Job Evaluation and Comparable Worth* (England: Gower Publishing, 1987).

4. U.S. General Accounting Office, *Description of Selected Nonfederal Job Evaluation Systems* (Washington, D.C.: GAO, 1985b).

5. Treiman, *Job Evaluation: An Analytic Review.*

6. Donald J. Treiman and Heidi I. Hartmann, eds., *Women, Work, and Wages: Equal Pay for Jobs of Equal Value* (Washington, D.C.: National Academy Press, 1981).

7. Treiman and Hartmann, *Women, Work, and Wages,* 83.

8. See for example, Joan Acker, *Doing Comparable Worth* (Philadelphia: Temple University Press, 1989); Helen Remick, *Comparable Worth and Wage Discrimination* (Philadelphia: Temple University Press, 1984); and Ronnie Steinberg and Lois Haignere, "Equitable Compensation: Methodological Criteria for Comparable Worth," in *Ingredients for Women's Employment Policy,* ed. Christine Bose and Glenna Spitze (New York: State University of New York Press, 1987).

9. Treiman, *Job Evaluation: An Analytic Review*; and Treiman and Hartmann, *Women, Work, and Wages.*

10. Robert M. Madigan and Frederick S. Hills, "Job Evaluation and Pay Equity," *Public Personnel Management* 17 (Fall 1988): 323–30; Donald P. Schwab, "Using Job Evaluation to Obtain Pay Equity," in *Comparable Worth: Issue for the 80's* vol. 1, ed. U.S. Commission on Civil Rights (Washington, D.C.: U.S. Commission on Civil Rights, 1984), 83–92.

11. Treiman, *Job Evaluation: An Analytic Review.*

12. Leslie Zebrowitz McArthur, "Social Judgment Biases in Comparable Worth Analysis," in *Comparable Worth: New Directions for Research,* ed. Heidi I. Hartmann (Washington, D.C.: National Academy Press, 1985).

13. Donald P. Schwab, "Job Evaluation Research and Research Needs," in *Comparable Worth: New Directions for Research,* ed. Heidi I. Hartmann (Washington, D.C.: National Academy Press, 1985), 37–52.

14. Treiman, *Job Evaluation: An Analytic Review.*

15. Schwab, "Job Evaluation Research and Research Needs."

16. Ibid.

17. Madigan and Hills, "Job Evaluation and Pay Equity."

18. Mary Witt and Patricia K. Naherny, *Women's Work: Up From .878* (Wisconsin: University of Wisconsin Extension, 1975).

19. Mary Anne McKellar, *Pay Equity Reports* vol. 2 (Ontario: Pay Equity Hearings Tribunal, 1991), 129.

20. Ibid., 122.

21. Steinberg and Haignere, "Equitable Compensation"; Witt and Naherny, *Women's Work: Up From .878.*

22. Acker, *Doing Comparable Worth.*

23. Barbara Bergmann, "Pay Equity—Surprising Answers to Hard Questions," *Challenge* 30 (May/June 1987): 45–51; Ronnie Steinberg, "'A Want of Harmony': Perspectives on Wage Discrimination and Comparable Worth," in *Comparable Worth and Wage Discrimination,* ed. Helen Remick (Philadelphia: Temple University Press, 1984); Treiman, *Job Evaluation: An Analytic Review.*

24. For other examples, see Henry Aaron and Cameran Lougy, *The Comparable Worth Controversy* (Washington, D.C.: The Brookings Institution, 1986).

25. Ronald G. Ehrenberg and Robert S. Smith, "Comparable Worth in the Public Sector," in *Public Sector Payrolls,* ed. David A. Wise (Chicago: University of Chicago Press, 1987).

26. Acker, *Doing Comparable Worth*; Elaine Johansen, *Comparable Worth: The Myth and the Movement* (Boulder, Colo.: Westview Press, Inc. 1984); Sara M. Evans and Barbara J. Nelson, *Wage Justice: Comparable Worth and the Paradox of Technocratic Reform* (Chicago: University of Chicago Press, 1989).

27. This example is given by Wisconsin's Task Force on Comparable Worth to explain how their approach differs from other efforts like that in Minnesota. Wisconsin Task Force on Comparable Worth, *Report of Wisconsin's Task Force on Comparable Worth* (1986).

28. National Committee on Pay Equity, *Pay Equity Activity in the Public Sector: 1979–1989* (Washington, D.C.: NCPE, 1989).

29. Johansen, *Comparable Worth: The Myth and the Movement.*

30. Keon S. Chi, "Comparable Worth in State Government: Trends and Issues," *Policy Studies Review* 5:4 (May 1986), 800–13.

31. Ibid.

32. Ibid.

33. Evans and Nelson, *Wage Justice.*

34. Johansen, *Comparable Worth: The Myth and the Movement*; Evans and Nelson, *Wage Justice*; Karolyn L. Godbey, "Predicting the Adoption of Comparable Worth Policies in the United States," in *Second Annual Women's Policy Research Conference Proceedings,* ed. Institute for Women's Policy Research (IWPR) (Washington, D.C.: IWPR, 1990).

35. Godbey, "Predicting the Adoption of Comparable Worth Policies."

36. Evans and Nelson, *Wage Justice.*

37. Ronald G. Ehrenberg and Robert S. Smith, *Modern Labor Economics: Theory and Public Policy*, 2d ed. (Illinois: Scott, Foresman, 1985).

38. B.V.H. Schneider, "Public-Sector Labor Legislation—An Evolutionary Analysis," in *Public-Sector Bargaining*, 2d ed., ed. Benjamin Aaron, Joyce M. Najita, and James L. Stern (Washington, D.C.: Bureau of National Affairs, Inc., 1988), 189–228.

39. John F. Burton, Jr., and Terry Thomason, "The Extent of Collective Bargaining in the Public Sector," in *Public-Sector Bargaining*, 2d ed., ed. Benjamin Aaron, Joyce M. Najita, and James L. Stern (Washington, D.C.: Bureau of National Affairs, Inc. 1988), 1–52.

40. Evans and Nelson, *Wage Justice*, 180–82.

41. Johansen, *Comparable Worth: The Myth and the Movement*.

42. Ibid.

43. Ibid.

44. Ibid.

45. Ibid.

46. Evans and Nelson, *Wage Justice*.

47. Godbey, "Predicting the Adoption of Comparable Worth Policies"; Johansen, *Comparable Worth: The Myth and the Movement*.

48. Jack L. Walker, "The Diffusion of Innovations Among the American States," *The American Political Science Review* 63 (1969): 880–99.

49. Godbey, "Predicting the Adoption of Comparable Worth Policies."

50. Johansen, *Comparable Worth: The Myth and the Movement*.

51. Johansen, *Comparable Worth: The Myth and the Movement*; Evans and Nelson, *Wage Justice*.

52. Susan Bucknell, "The Connecticut Story on Objective Job Evaluation," in *Manual on Pay Equity*, ed. Joy Ann Grune (Washington, D.C.: Conference on Alternative State and Local Policies, 1979).

53. National Committee on Pay Equity, *Pay Equity Activity in the Public Sector: 1979–1989*.

54. Acker, *Doing Comparable Worth*, 174.

55. Dennis L. Dresang, "The Politics of Pay Equity in Wisconsin," University of Wisconsin, Madison, mimeo.

56. Acker, *Doing Comparable Worth*; Johansen, *Comparable Worth: The Myth and the Movement*.

57. Acker, *Doing Comparable Worth*; Ronnie J. Steinberg, "Job Evaluation and Managerial Control: The Politics of Technique and the Techniques of Politics," in *Just Wages: A Feminist Assessment of Pay Equity*, ed. Judy Fudge and Patricia McDermott (Toronto: University of Toronto Press, 1992).

58. Oregon Senate Bill No. 484, approved by the governor in August 1983.

59. Acker, *Doing Comparable Worth*, 42.

60. Ibid., 188.

61. This cost estimate is from Peter F. Orazem and J. Peter Mattila, "The Implementation Process of Comparable Worth: Winners and Losers," *Journal of Political Economy* 98 (1990): 137.

CHAPTER FIVE

1. Robert S. Smith, "Comparable Worth: Limited Coverage and the Exacerbation of Inequality," *Industrial and Labor Relations Review* 2 (1988).

2. Ronald G. Ehrenberg and Robert S. Smith, "Comparable Worth in the Public Sector," in *Public Sector Payrolls*, ed. David A. Wise (Chicago: University of Chicago Press, 1987); Elaine Sorensen, "Implementing Comparable Worth: A Survey of Recent Job Evaluation Studies," *American Economic Review* 76 (1986); Elaine Sorensen, "The Effect of Comparable Worth Policies on Earnings," *Industrial Relations* 26 (1987).

3. Peter F. Orazem and J. Peter Mattila, "The Implementation Process of Comparable Worth: Winners and Losers," *Journal of Political Economy* 98 (1990).

4. June O'Neill, Michael Brien, and James Cunningham, "Effects of Comparable Worth Policy: Evidence From Washington State," *American Economic Review* 79 (1989).

5. Mark R. Killingsworth, *The Economics of Comparable Worth* (Kalamazoo, Mich.: W.E. Upjohn Institute, 1990).

6. O'Neill et al., "Effects of Comparable Worth Policy."

7. Killingsworth, *The Economics of Comparable Worth*.

8. Ronald G. Ehrenberg and Robert S. Smith, "Comparable Worth Wage Adjustments and Female Employment in the State and Local Sector," *Journal of Labor Economics* 5 (April 1987).

9. O'Neill et al., "Effects of Comparable Worth Policy."

10. Killingsworth, *The Economics of Comparable Worth*.

11. O'Neill et al., "Effects of Comparable Worth Policy."

12. Killingsworth, *The Economics of Comparable Worth*.

13. Minnesota Commission on the Economic Status of Women, *Pay Equity: The Minnesota Experience* (Minnesota: Minnesota Commission on the Economic Status of Women, 1989).

14. I thank Mark Killingsworth for giving me a copy of the first nineteen quarters of this data. The final ten quarters were purchased from the Minnesota State Department of Employee Relations.

15. The state of Minnesota originally targeted only female-dominated jobs for comparable worth wage adjustments, but some of these jobs changed to integrated jobs during the four years of comparable worth implementation, explaining the 2 percent figure.

16. The complete regression results are reported in Appendix Table 5A.2.

17. Some might argue that the results from two cross-sectional analyses before and after comparable worth may be influenced by changes in the composition of the work force that are not controlled for in the analysis and may reflect exogenous factors that are not taken into account in the analysis (see for example Orazem and Mattila, "The Implementation Process of Comparable Worth: Winners and Losers," 138). According to this view, one can not attribute the dramatic decline in the (absolute value of the) coefficient for the "femaleness" of the occupation to comparable worth. While it is possible that these other factors contributed to the decline in the coefficient, it is difficult to believe they virtually eliminated its negative effect on earnings, which occurred during the implementation of comparable worth. The size of the decline certainly suggests that comparable worth contributed to its reduction. Critics of the pre- and post-snapshot approach will hopefully be persuaded by the fixed-effects regressions presented below.

18. Since there are so many individuals in the analysis, dummy variables for each individual are not, in fact, added to the regression equation. Instead, I express each variable in the analysis in terms of deviations from the individual means and run a least squares regression without the constant term. This approach yields the same estimated slope coefficients as the dummy variable model. See Judge, Hill, Griffiths, Lutkepohl, and Lee (1988, 472) for greater details.

19. I selected this representative sample by selecting a random sample of employees from the entire population of workers employed by the state of Minnesota during the period of analysis. More specifically, I took a random sample of (scrambled) social security numbers from the set of all unique social security numbers that existed between October 1981 and October 1988. Once this random sample of individuals was selected, I went back to the original personnel records and retrieved all of the available data for these randomly selected individuals.

20. Some workers move from a targeted job to one that is not targeted by comparable worth during their tenure with the state. Measuring the effect of comparable worth on these individuals is more difficult. Thus, once I examined the effects of comparable worth on workers in targeted and non-targeted jobs, I selected workers who either remained in a targeted job throughout their state service or who always worked in a nontargeted job for the state. This allowed me to isolate the effect of comparable worth from other changes in earnings that result from job mobility in and out of targeted jobs. I excluded 12 percent of the work force by limiting my analysis in this manner.

21. Real hourly pay is equal to nominal hourly pay multiplied by the ratio of the current price index in October 1988 to the current price index in the month of the data.

22. The Minnesota personnel data do not include information about a

person's total work experience with the state. They only include a person's current employment tenure. In other words, a person may have worked for the state of Minnesota for twenty years, left for a year, and then come back. The personnel data would report the most recent date of entry to state service for this person. Thus, the person's twenty years of service prior to the most recent period would not be reflected in the current record.

23. Women's percentage change in pay is equal to $\exp(a)-1$, where a is the sum of the estimated coefficients for the comparable worth indicator variables in the women's wage equation reported in the final page of Table 5A.4.

24. The percentage change in women's relative pay is equal to $\exp(a-b)-1$, where a and b are the sum of the estimated coefficients for the comparable worth indicator variables in the women's and men's wage equations, respectively, reported in the final page of Table 5A.4.

25. The increase in the female-to-male pay ratio that results from comparable worth is equal to the female-to-male pay ratio before comparable worth multiplied by $\exp(a-b)$, where a and b are the sum of the estimated coefficients for the comparable worth indicator variables in the women's and men's wage equations, respectively, reported in the final page of Table 5A.4.

26. This elementary demand function is derived from a constant elasticity of substitution (CES) cost function (Hamermesh 1986). The typical labor demand function derived from a CES cost function is:

$$\ln N_{jt} = b_0 + b_1 \ln w_{jt} + b_2 \ln Y_t + v_{jt}$$

where Y is total output. I have assumed that the X vector in the equation in the text is a proxy for output. Thus, the coefficient on the wage variable should be interpreted as an output-constant wage elasticity that does not incorporate output (or "scale") effects.

27. Killingsworth noted this in his analysis of employment demand. Killingsworth, *The Economics of Comparable Worth*, 91.

28. $3.9 = -.165$ (the wage elasticity for targeted jobs) * 23.6 (the percent increase in women's pay in targeted jobs resulting from comparable worth).

29. $0.3 = -.62$ (the wage elasticity for nontargeted jobs) * .5 (the percent increase in women's pay in nontargeted jobs resulting from comparable worth).

30. $2.6 = (3.9 * .65) + (.3 * .35)$, where .65 and .35 are the proportion of women working, on average, in targeted and nontargeted jobs, respectively.

31. $3.0 = -.165$ (the wage elasticity for targeted jobs) * 18.3 (the percent increase in men's pay in targeted jobs resulting from comparable worth); $0.7 = -.62$ (the wage elasticity for nontargeted jobs) * 1.2 (the percent increase in men's pay in nontargeted jobs resulting from comparable worth).

32. $0.9 = (.74 * .93) + (3.0 * .07)$, where .93 and .07 are the proportion of men working, on average, in nontargeted and targeted jobs, respectively.

33. Elaine Sorensen, "Wage and Employment Effects of Pay Equity: Evidence from the United States," in *Policy Forum on Pay Equity: Means and Ends*, ed. Michael G. Abbott (Queens University, Ontario: John Deutsch Institute for the Study of Economic Policy, 1990), 33–47. For further details, see Elaine Sorensen, "Wage and Employment Effects of Comparable Worth: The Case of Minnesota," Urban Institute Working Paper, 1990.

34. Killingsworth, *The Economics of Comparable Worth*.

35. More recently, Killingsworth has examined all four comparable worth adjustments in Minnesota, but I was unable to replicate these more recent results. See Mark R. Killingsworth, "Benefits and Costs of Comparable Worth," in *Policy Forum on Pay Equity: Means and Ends*, ed. Michael G. Abbott (Queens University, Kingston Ontario: John Deutsch Institute for the Study of Economic Policy, 1990), 47–62. In his new study, Killingsworth divided workers into those who worked in jobs targeted by comparable worth and those who did not work in these jobs. But he did not explain how he defined these groups. Workers move in and out of targeted jobs, so it is unclear how he divided workers into these two groups. Because I lacked this information, I was unable to replicate his more recent results. My own efforts to divide these workers, which were presented above, led to very different results than those of Killingsworth. Nonetheless, his new work still suffers from the other problems that affected his earlier work, which I discuss below.

36. Killingsworth, *The Economics of Comparable Worth*, 130. This is Killingsworth's basic fixed-effects earnings regression for the Minnesota data. He presents results from two other fixed-effects analyses of wages. The first has measures of private wage growth rather than the time trend and its square. The second model has measures of both private wage growth and the time trend variables.

37. As I explained earlier, the Minnesota personnel data do not include information about a person's total work experience with the state. They only include a person's current employment tenure. Killingsworth attempted to use the longitudinal nature of the data to capture more of a person's tenure with the state than is reflected in the current record (Killingsworth, *The Economics of Comparable Worth*, 136). In his fixed-effects model, he used a person's earliest date of entry to state service reported in the data to calculate employment tenure rather than the current entry date. I constructed this measure to replicate Killingsworth's work that is presented below.

38. The price variables for October 1981, for example, reflect the CPI in September, June, and March 1981, and December 1980.

39. Killingsworth sets TIME equal to zero in January 1960. Our different reference points for the time variable will result in different estimated coefficients on TIME and TIMESQ, but it will not affect the estimated coefficients for the comparable worth variables.

40. Killingsworth, *The Economics of Comparable Worth*, 128. Killingsworth reports percentage point changes that result from pay equity. I have converted these to percentage changes.

41. My results are slightly different from Killingsworth. This difference may be caused by the fact that I do not limit my analysis to white workers as Killingsworth did.

42. Killingsworth also estimated a labor demand function for jobs that were neither male- nor female-dominated, but these estimates are less relevant to my discussion, so I do not discuss these results.

43. Killingsworth also used two other measures of the wage variables—the minimum and maximum wage rates available in each job—but these definitions of pay are less satisfactory than the mean wage. Thus, I focus my analysis on the mean wage.

44. All variables used in the fixed-effects analysis are defined in appendix table 5A.1.

45. I am not sure why I was unable to replicate Killingsworth's results. The steps I took to reproduce his work are as follows: (1) I fixed any missing or changing sex in the twenty-nine quarters of data; (2) I created occupation-level data sets from the original personnel data, which included the mean value of the logarithm of employment and wages for the first nineteen quarters; (3) I determined the sex composition of the occupations in October 1981; (4) I added the time trend and price control variables to these data files; (5) I limited the sample to occupations that had positive employment in all 19 quarters; and (6) I combined these data and determined the mean value for the variables in the analysis for each job category and subtracted this mean from the actual values.

46. Real wages are defined as before (see footnote 21 above).

CHAPTER SIX

1. Bureau of National Affairs, *Pay Equity and Comparable Worth* (Washington, D.C.: BNA, 1984).

2. Walter Oi, "Neglected Women and Other Implications of Comparable Worth," *Contemporary Policy Issues* 4 (1986): 21–32; Robert S. Smith, "Comparable Worth: Limited Coverage and the Exacerbation of Inequality," *Industrial and Labor Relations Review* 41 (1988): 227–39.

❖ *References* ❖

Aaron, Henry, and Cameran Lougy. *The Comparable Worth Controversy.* Washington, D.C.: The Brookings Institution, 1986.

Acker, Joan. *Doing Comparable Worth.* Philadelphia: Temple University Press, 1989.

Aldrich, Mark, and Robert Buchele. *The Economics of Comparable Worth.* Cambridge, Mass.: Ballinger, 1986.

Arthur Young and Co. *Study to Establish an Evaluation System for State of Iowa Merit Employment System Classifications on the Basis of Comparable Worth.* New York: Arthur young and Company, 1984.

———. *The Decision Band Method.* New York: Arthur Young and Company, 1985.

———. *A Job Evaluation Study of Selected Job Classes of the State and Counties of Hawaii.* New York: Arthur Young and Company, 1987.

Averitt, Robert T. *The Dual Economy: The Dynamics of American Industry Structure.* New York: W. W. Norton, 1968.

Beck, E. M., Patrick M. Horan, and Charles M. Tolbert, II. "Stratification in a Dual Economy: A Sectoral Model of Earnings Determination." *American Sociological Review* 43 (October 1978): 704–20.

Becker, Gary. *The Economics of Discrimination.* Chicago: University of Chicago Press, 1957 (2d ed., 1971).

Beller, Andrea H. "Occupational Segregation by Sex: Determinants and Changes." *Journal of Human Resources* 17 (1982): 371–92.

———. "Trends in Occupational Segregation by Sex and Race, 1960–1981." In *Sex Segregation in the Workplace,* ed. Barbara F. Reskin, 11–26. Washington, D.C.: National Academy Press, 1984.

———. "Occupational Segregation and the Earnings Gap." In *Comparable Worth: Issue for the 80's,* vol. 1, ed. U.S. Commission on Civil Rights, 23–33. Washington, D.C.: U.S. Commission on the Civil Rights, 1984.

Bergmann, Barbara R. "Occupational Segregation, Wages and Profits When Employers Discriminate by Race and Sex." *Eastern Economic Journal* 1 (April/July 1974): 103–10.

———. "Pay Equity—Surprising Answers to Hard Questions." *Challenge* 30 (May/June 1987): 45–51.

Berndt, Ernst R., and David O. Wood. "Technology, Prices, and the Derived Demand for Energy." *The Review of Economics and Statistics* 57 (August 1975): 259–68.

153

Bianchi, Suzanne M., and Daphne Spain. *American Women in Transition*. New York: Russell Sage Foundation, 1986.

Bielby, William T., and James N. Baron. "A Woman's Place Is with Other Women: Sex Segregation Within Organizations." In *Sex Segregation in the Workplace*, ed. Barbara F. Reskin, 27–55. Washington, D.C.: National Academy Press, 1984.

Blau, Francine D. "Occupational Segregation and Labor Market Discrimination." In *Sex Segregation in the Workplace*, ed. Barbara F. Reskin, 117–43. Washington, D.C.: National Academy Press, 1984.

Blau, Francine D., and Andrea H. Beller, "Trends in Earnings Differentials by Gender, 1971–1981." *Industrial and Labor Relations Review* 41 (1988): 513–29.

Blau, Francine D., and Marianne A. Ferber. "Discrimination: Empirical Evidence from the United States." *American Economic Review* 77 (1987): 316–20.

Blau, Francine D., and Carol Jusenius. "Economists' Approaches to Sex Segregation in the Labor Market: An Appraisal." In *Women and the Workplace: The Implications of Occupational Segregation*. ed. Martha Blaxall and Barbara Reagan, 181–99. Chicago: University of Chicago Press, 1976.

Brown, Charles. "Equalizing Differences in the Labor Market." *The Quarterly Journal of Economics* (February 1980): 113–34.

Bucknell, Susan. "The Connecticut Story on Objective Job Evaluation." In *Manual on Pay Equity*, ed. Joy Ann Grune. Washington, D.C.: Conference on Alternative State and Local Policies, 1979.

Bureau of National Affairs. *The Comparable Worth Issue*. Washington, D.C.: Bureau of National Affairs, 1981.

———. *Pay Equity and Comparable Worth*. Washington, D.C.: Bureau of National Affairs, 1984.

Burton, John F., Jr., and Terry Thomason. "The Extent of Collective Bargaining in the Public Sector." In *Public Sector Bargaining*, 2d ed., ed. Benjamin Aaron, Joyce M. Najita, and James L. Stern, 1–51. Washington, D.C.: Bureau of National Affairs, 1988.

Cain, Glen G. "The Economic Analysis of Labor Market Discrimination: A Survey." In *Handbook of Labor Economics* 1, ed. Orley Ashenfelter and Richard Layard, 693–785. Netherlands: Elsevier Science, 1986.

Chi, Keon S. "Comparable Worth in State Government: Trends and Issues." *Policy Studies Review* 5 (May 1986): 800–813.

Doeringer, Peter B., and Michael J. Piore. *Internal Labor Markets and Manpower Analysis*. Massachusetts: D.C. Heath and Company, 1971.

Dresang, Dennis L. "The Politics of Pay Equity in Wisconsin." Wisconsin: University of Wisconsin, mimeo.

Ehrenberg, Ronald G. "Empirical Consequences of Comparable Worth." In *Comparable Worth: Analyses and Evidence*, ed. M. Anne Hill and Mark R. Killingsworth, 90–106. Ithaca, New York: ILR Press, 1989.

Ehrenberg, Ronald G., and Robert S. Smith. *Modern Labor Economics: Theory and Public Policy*, 2d ed. Glenview, Ill.: Scott, Foresman, 1985.

————. "Comparable Worth in the Public Sector." In *Public Sector Payrolls*, ed. David A. Wise. Chicago: University of Chicago Press, 1987.

————. "Comparable Worth Wage Adjustments and Female Employment in the State and Local Sector." *Journal of Labor Economics* 5 (April 1987): 43–62.

Elizur, Dov. *Systematic Job Evaluation and Comparable Worth*. Bar Llan University, and Israel Institute of Applied Social Research. England: Gower Publishing, 1987.

England, Paula. "The Failure of Human Capital Theory to Explain Occupational Sex Segregation." *Journal of Human Resources* 17 (1982): 358–70.

————. *Comparable Worth: Theories and Evidence*. New York: Walter de Gruyter, 1992.

England, Paula, Marilyn Chassie, and Linda McCormack. "Skill Demands and Earnings in Female and Male Occupations." *Sociology and Social Research* 66 (1982): 147–68.

England, Paula, George Farkas, Barbara Kilbourne, and Thomas Dou. "Explaining Occupational Segregation and Wages: Findings from a Model with Fixed Effects." *American Sociological Review* 53 (1988): 544–58.

Evans, Sara M., and Barbara J. Nelson. *Wage Justice: Comparable Worth and the Paradox of Technocratic Reform*. Chicago: University of Chicago Press, 1989.

Ferber, Marianne A., and Helen M. Lowry. "The Sex Differential in Earnings: A Reappraisal." *Industrial and Labor Relations Review* 29 (1976): 377–87.

Filer, Randall. "Occupational Segregation, Compensating Differentials and Comparable Worth." In *Pay Equity: Empirical Inquiries*, ed. Robert T. Michael et al., 153–70. Washington, D.C.: National Academy Press, 1989.

Gerhart, Barry, and Nabil El Cheikh. "Earnings and Percentage Female: A Longitudinal Study." *Industrial Relations* 30 (1990): 62–78.

Godbey, Karolyn L. "Predicting the Adoption of Comparable Worth Policies in the United States." In *Second Annual Women's Policy Research Conference Proceedings*, 190–94. Washington, D.C.: Institute for Women's Policy Research, 1990.

Gregory, R. G., and A. E. Daly. "Can Economic Theory Explain Why Australian Women Are So Well Paid Relative to their U.S. Counterparts?" Mimeo. Australia: Centre for Economic Policy Research at the Australian National University, 1991.

Gregory, R. G., and R. C. Duncan. "Segmented Labor Market Theories and the Australian Experience of Equal Pay for Women." *Journal of Post Keynesian Economics* 3 (1981): 403–28.

Gregory, Robert G., Roslyn Anstie, Anne Daly, and Vivian Ho. "Women's Pay in Australia, Great Britain, and the United States: The Role of Laws, Regulations, and Human Capital." In *Pay Equity: Empirical Inquiries*, eds. Robert T. Michael et al., 222–42. Washington, D.C.: National Academy Press, 1989.

Gunderson, Morley. "Implementation of Comparable Worth in Canada." *Journal of Social Issues* 45 (1989): 209–22.

Hamermesh, Daniel S. "The Demand for Labor in the Long Run." In *Handbook of Labor Economics* vol. 1, ed. Orley C. Ashenfelter and Richard Layard. Netherlands: Elsevier Science, 1986.

Hartmann, Heidi I., ed. *Comparable Worth: New Directions for Research*. Washington, D.C.: National Academy Press, 1985.

Johansen, Elaine. *Comparable Worth: The Myth and the Movement*. Boulder, Colo.: Westview Press, 1984.

Johnson, George, and Gary Solon. "Pay Differences Between Women's and Men's Jobs: The Empirical Foundations of Comparable Worth Legislation." National Bureau of Economic Research, Working Paper No. 1472, 1984.

———. "Estimates of the Direct Effects of Comparable Worth Policy." *American Economic Review* 76 (1986): 1117–25.

Judge, George C., R. Carter Hill, William E. Griffiths, Helmut Lutkepohl, and Tsoung-Chao Lee. *Introduction to the Theory and Practice of Econometrics*, 2d ed. New York: John Wiley and Sons, 1988.

Kahn, Shulamit. "Economic Implications of Public Sector Comparable Worth: A Case Study of San Jose." Mimeo. University of California, Irvine, 1987.

Kelly, Rita Mae, and Jane Baynes, eds. *Comparable Worth, Pay Equity and Public Policy*. Westport, Conn.: Greenwood Press, 1988.

Killingsworth, Mark R. "Heterogeneous Preferences, Compensating Wage Differentials, and Comparable Worth." *Quarterly Journal of Economics* CII (November 1987): 727–42.

———. *The Economics of Comparable Worth*. Kalamazoo: W. E. Upjohn Institute, 1990.

———. "Benefits and Costs of Comparable Worth." In *Policy Forum on Pay Equity: Means and Ends*, ed. Michael G. Abbott, 47–62. Kingston, Ontario: John Deutsch Institute for the Study of Economic Policy, 1990.

Levitan, Sar A., Peter E. Carlson, and Isaac Shapiro. *Protecting American Workers*. Washington, D.C.: Bureau of National Affairs, 1986.

Lewis, Gregory B., and Mark A. Emmert. "The Sexual Division of Labor in Federal Employment." *Social Science Quarterly* 67 (March 1986): 143–55.

Livernash, Robert E., ed. *Comparable Worth: Issues and Alternatives.* Washington, D.C.: Equal Employment Advisory Council, 1980.

Livy, Brian. *Job Evaluation: A Critical Review.* New York: John Wiley and Sons, 1975.

Madigan Robert M., and Frederick S. Hills, "Job Evaluation and Pay Equity." *Public Personnel Management* 17 (Fall 1988): 323–30.

Marshall, Ray, and Beth Paulin. "The Employment and Earnings of Women: The Comparable Worth Debate." In *Comparable Worth: Issue for the 80's,* vol. 1, ed. U.S. Commission on Civil Rights. Washington, D.C.: U.S. Commission on Civil Rights, 1984.

Massachusetts Special Committee on Comparable Worth. *Third (Interim) Report,* 1988.

McArthur, Leslie Zebrowitz. "Social Judgment Biases in Comparable Worth Analysis." In *Comparable Worth: New Directions for Research,* ed. Heidi I. Hartmann, 53–70. Washington, D.C.: National Academy Press, 1985.

McDermott, Patricia. "Pay Equity in Canada: Assessing the Commitment to Reducing the Wage Gap." In *Just Wages: A Feminist Assessment of Pay Equity,* eds. Judy Fudge and Patricia McDermott, 21–32. Toronto: University of Toronto Press, 1991.

McKellar, Mary Anne, ed. *Pay Equity Reports,* vol. 2. Ontario: Pay Equity Hearings Tribunal, 1991.

Michael, Robert T., Heidi I. Hartmann, and Brigid O'Farrell, eds. *Pay Equity: Empirical Inquiries.* Washington, D.C.: National Research Council, 1989.

Miller, Ann R., Donald J. Treiman, Pamela S. Cain, and Patricia A. Roos, eds. *Work, Jobs, and Occupations: A Critical Review of the Dictionary of Occupational Titles.* Washington, D.C.: National Academy Press, 1980.

Minnesota Commission on the Economic Status of Women. "Pay Equity and Public Employment." Minnesota: Minnesota Commission on the Economic Status of Women, 1982.

―――. *Pay Equity: The Minnesota Experience.* Minnesota: Minnesota Commission on the Economic Status of Women, 1989.

Minnesota Department of Employee Relations. "Hay Point Ratings for State of Minnesota Jobs." Minnesota: Minnesota Department of Employee Relations, 1984.

National Committee on Pay Equity. *Closing the Wage Gap: An International Perspective.* Washington, D.C.: National Committee on Pay Equity, 1988.

National Committee on Pay Equity. *Pay Equity Activity in the Public Sector: 1979–1989.* Washington, D.C.: National Committee on Pay Equity, 1989.

———. *Legislating Pay Equity.* Washington, D.C.: National Committee on Pay Equity, 1990.

———. *Newsnotes,* vol. 12, no. 1. Washington, D.C.: National Committee on Pay Equity, 1991.

Oaxaca, Ronald. "Male-Female Wage Differentials in Urban Labor Markets." *International Economic Review* 14 (1973): 693–709.

Oi, Walter. "Neglected Women and Other Implications of Comparable Worth." *Contemporary Policy Issues* 4 (1986): 21–32.

O'Neill, June. "The Determinants and Wage Effects of Occupational Segregation." The Urban Institute, 1983.

———. "An Argument Against Comparable Worth." In *Comparable Worth: Issue for the 80's,* vol. 1, ed. U.S. Commission on Civil Rights, 177–86. Washington, D.C.: U.S. Commission on Civil Rights, 1984.

O'Neill, June, Michael Brien, and James Cunningham. "Effects of Comparable Worth Policy: Evidence From Washington State." *American Economic Review* 79 (May 1989): 305–09.

Orazem, Peter F., and Peter J. Mattila. "Comparable Worth and the Structure of Earnings: The Iowa Case." In *Pay Equity: Empirical Inquiries,* ed. Robert T. Michael et al., 179–99. Washington, D.C.: National Academy Press, 1989.

———. "The Implementation of Comparable Worth: Winners and Losers." *Journal of Political Economy* 98 (February 1990): 134–52.

Oregon Task Force on State Compensation and Classification Equity. *Final Report and Recommendations,* 1985.

Pinzler, Isabelle Katz, and Deborah Ellis. "Wage Discrimination and Comparable Worth: A Legal Perspective." *Journal of Social Issues* 45 (1989): 51–66.

Polachek, Solomon William. "Women in the Economy: Perspectives on Gender Inequality." In *Comparable Worth: Issue for the 80's,* vol. 1, ed. U.S. Commission on Civil Rights, 34–53. Washington, D.C.: U.S. Commission on Civil Rights, 1984.

Public Opinion. "Comparable Worth: Public Uninformed and Skeptical." *Public Opinion* (October 1986): 34–35.

Remick, Helen. "Major Issues in A Priori Applications." In *Comparable Worth and Wage Discrimination,* ed. Helen Remick, 99–117. Philadelphia: Temple University Press, 1984.

———, ed. *Comparable Worth and Wage Discrimination.* Philadelphia: Temple University Press, 1984.

Robb, Roberta. "Equal Pay for Work of Equal Value in Ontario: An Overview." In *Policy Forum on Pay Equity: Means and Ends,* ed. Michael G.

Abbott, 16–20. Queens University, Kingston, Ontario: John Deutsch Institute for the Study of Economic Policy, 1990.

Schafly, Phyllis, ed. *Equal Pay for UNequal Work*. Washington, D.C.: Eagle Forum Education and Legal Defense Fund, 1984.

Scheibal, William. "AFSCME v. Washington: The Continued Viability of Title VII Comparable Worth Actions." *Public Personnel Management* 17 (Fall 1988): 315–22.

Schneider, B.V.H. "Public-Sector Labor Legislation—An Evolutionary Analysis." In *Public Sector Bargaining*, 2d ed., ed. Benjamin Aaron, Joyce M. Najita, and James L. Stern, 189–228. Washington, D.C.: Bureau of National Affairs.

Schwab, Donald P. "Using Job Evaluation to Obtain Pay Equity." In *Comparable Worth: Issue for the 80's*, vol. 1, ed. U.S. Commission on Civil Rights, 83–92. Washington, D.C.: U.S. Commission on Civil Rights, 1984.

———. "Job Evaluation Research and Research Needs." In *Comparable Worth: New Directions for Research*, ed. Heidi I. Hartmann, 37–52. Washington, D.C.: National Academy Press, 1985.

Smith, Robert S. "Comparable Worth: Limited Coverage and the Exacerbation of Inequality." *Industrial and Labor Relations Review* 41 (1988): 227–39.

Smith, Shirley J. "New Worklife Estimates Reflect Changing Profile of Labor Force." *Monthly Labor Review* (March 1982): 15–20.

Snyder, David, and Paula M. Hudis. "The Sex Differential in Earnings: A Further Reappraisal." *Industrial and Labor Relations Review* 32 (1979): 378–84.

Sorensen, Elaine. "Implementing Comparable Worth: A Survey of Recent Job Evaluation Studies." *American Economic Review* 76 (May 1986): 364–67.

———. "The Effect of Comparable Worth Policies on Earnings." *Industrial Relations* 26 (1987): 227–39.

———. "Measuring the Effect of Occupational Sex and Race Composition on Earnings." In *Pay Equity: Empirical Inquiries*, ed. Robert T. Michael et al., 101–24. Washington, D.C.: National Academy Press, 1989.

———. "Measuring the Pay Disparity Between Typically Female Occupations and Other Jobs: A Bivariate Selectivity Approach." *Industrial and Labor Relations Review* 42 (July 1989): 634–39.

———. "The Crowding Hypothesis and Comparable Worth Issue." *Journal of Human Resources* 25 (Winter 1990): 55–89.

———. "Wage and Employment Effects of Pay Equity: Evidence from the United States." In *Policy Forum on Pay Equity: Means and Ends*, ed. Michael G. Abbott, 33–46. Kingston, Ontario: John Deutsch Institute for the Study of Economic Policy, 1990.

Sorensen, Elaine. "Wage and Employment Effects of Comparable Worth: The Case of Minnesota." Washington, D.C.: Urban Institute Working Paper, 1990.

Steinberg, Ronnie. "'A Want of Harmony': Perspectives on Wage Discrimination and Comparable Worth." In *Comparable Worth and Wage Discrimination*, ed. Helen Remick, 3–27. Philadelphia: Temple University Press, 1984.

————. "Job Evaluation and Managerial Control: The Politics of Technique and the Technique of Politics." In *Just Wages: A Feminist Assessment of Pay Equity*, ed. Judy Fudge and Patricia McDermott, 193–220. Toronto: University of Toronto Press, 1991.

Steinberg, Ronnie, and Lois Haignere. "Equitable Compensation: Methodological Criteria for Comparable Worth." In *Ingredients for Women's Employment Policy*, eds. Christine Bose and Glenna Spitze, 157–82. New York: State University of New York Press, 1987.

Tiegle, Christine. *The Development of a Quantitative Job Evaluation System for the State of New York: Methodology*, mimeo. 1987.

Treiman, Donald J. *Job Evaluation: An Analytic Review*. Washington, D.C.: National Academy of Sciences, 1979.

————. "Effect of Choice of Factors and Factor Weights in Job Evaluation." In *Comparable Worth and Wage Discrimination*, ed. Helen Remick, 79–89. Philadelphia: Temple University Press, 1984.

Treiman, Donald J., and Hartmann, Heidi I., eds. *Women, Work, and Wages: Equal Pay for Jobs of Equal Value*. Washington, D.C.: National Academy Press, 1981.

U.S. Bureau of the Census. "Detailed Occupation and Years of School Completed by Age for the Civilian Labor Force by Sex, Race, and Spanish Origin: 1980." PC80-S1-8. Washington, D.C.: U.S. Government Printing Office, 1983.

————. "1970–1980 Census Comparability: Chart B." unpublished, 1986.

————. "Male-Female Differences in Work Experience, Occupation, and Earnings: 1984." *Current Population Reports*, Series P-70, No. 10. Washington, D.C.: U.S. Government Printing Office, 1987.

U.S. Bureau of Labor Statistics. *Occupational Projections and Training Data*. Bulletin 2301. Washington, D.C.: U.S. Government Printing Office, 1988.

U.S. Commission on Civil Rights. *Comparable Worth: Issue for the 80's*. 2 vols. Washington, D.C.: U.S. Commission on Civil Rights, 1984.

U.S. General Accounting Office. *Description of Selected Systems for Classifying Federal Civilian Positions and Personnel*. Washington, D.C.: GAO, 1984.

————. *Distribution of Male and Female Employees in Four Federal Classification Systems*. Washington, D.C.: GAO, 1984.

REFERENCES

———. *Options for Conducting a Pay Equity Study of Federal Pay and Classification Systems*. Washington, D.C.: GAO, 1985.

———. *Description of Selected Nonfederal Job Evaluation Systems*. Washington, D.C.: GAO, 1985.

———. *Pay Equity: Status of State Activities*. Washington, D.C.: GAO, 1986.

———. *Pay Equity: Washington State's Efforts to Address Comparable Worth*. Washington, D.C.: GAO, 1992.

U.S. Office of Personnel Management. *Comparable Worth for Federal Jobs*. OPM Doc. 149-40-3. Washington, D.C.: OPM, 1987.

Walker, Jack L. "The Diffusion of Innovations among the American States." *The American Political Science Review* 63 (1969): 880–99.

Washington State Department of Personnel. *1984 Comparable Worth Study Report*, 1984.

Weiler, Paul. "The Wages of Sex: The Uses and Limits of Comparable Worth." *Harvard Law Review* 99 (1986): 1728–1807.

Wisconsin Task Force on Comparable Worth. *Report of Wisconsin's Task Force on Comparable Worth*, 1986.

Witt, Mary, and Patricia K. Naherny. *Women's Work: Up From .878*. Wisconsin: University of Wisconsin, Extension, 1975.

❖ Index ❖

166